SHIPS AND SHIPWRECKS

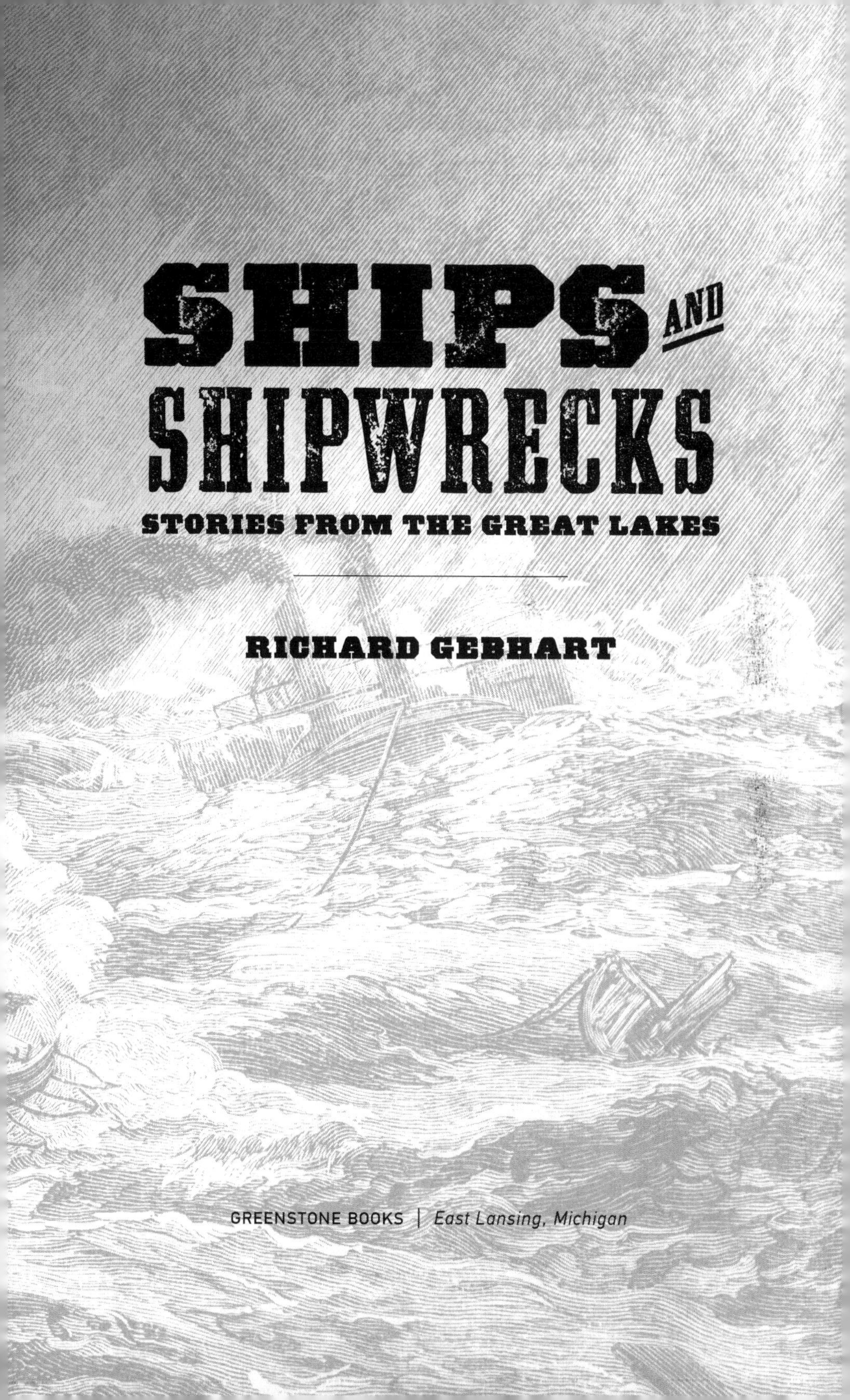

SHIPS AND SHIPWRECKS

STORIES FROM THE GREAT LAKES

RICHARD GEBHART

GREENSTONE BOOKS | *East Lansing, Michigan*

♾ The paper used in this publication meets the minimum requirements
of ANSI/NISO Z39.48-1992 (R 1997) (Permanence of Paper).

Greenstone Books is an imprint of Michigan State University Press.
The mission of Greenstone Books—a name chosen to evoke the state gem
of Michigan—is to publish works in history and environmental
studies accessible to a general readership.

Michigan State University Press
East Lansing, Michigan 48823-5245

LIBRARY OF CONGRESS CATALOGING-IN-PUBLICATION DATA
Names: Gebhart, Richard, author.
Title: Ships and shipwrecks : stories from the Great Lakes / Richard Gebhart.
Description: East Lansing : Michigan State University Press, [2021] |
Includes bibliographical references and index.
Identifiers: LCCN 2021001046 | ISBN 9781948314091 (paperback)
| ISBN 9781948314107 | ISBN 9781948314114 | ISBN 9781948314121
Subjects: LCSH: Ships—Great Lakes (North America)—History.
| Shipping—Great Lakes (North America)—History.
| Shipwrecks—Great Lakes (North America)—History.
| Sailors—Great Lakes (North America)—History.
| Great Lakes Region (North America)—Navigation—History.
Classification: LCC VK23.7 .G43 2021 | DDC 917.704—dc23
LC record available at https://lccn.loc.gov/2021001046

Book and cover design by Charlie Sharp, Sharp Des!gns, East Lansing, Michigan
Cover art: Steam vessel during a storm at sea 1895, by maodesign, from iStock.

Michigan State University Press is a member of the Green Press Initiative and is committed to developing and encouraging ecologically responsible publishing practices. For more information about the Green Press Initiative and the use of recycled paper in book publishing, please visit www.greenpressinitiative.org.

Visit Michigan State University Press at *www.msupress.org*

To the memory of those passed
who kindled my love of Great Lakes shipping history—
my dad, Uncle Archie, and mentor Edward N. Middleton—
who are not around to read this, but also those
who are my mom, sibs, family, and friends.

Contents

Preface

Historians accept that the *Griffon*, Robert Cavelier de La Salle's ship, was the first commercial vessel built by Europeans to sail on the Great Lakes. In the waning summer of 1679, on the return leg of its first trip, the *Griffon* disappeared. This was a harbinger of things to come over the next few centuries for vessels plying the Great Lakes. Many European and then American ships would follow in its wake, and some would disappear. The disappearance of the *Griffon* remains symbolic, although lost in the deep echoes of time.

In the centuries between the loss of the *Griffon* and the 1975 sinking of the celebrated *Edmund Fitzgerald*—memorialized in song by legendary folk singer Gordon Lightfoot—the records show that an alarming number of shipwrecks occurred on the Great Lakes. Exact numbers are not known. If one considers vessels that wrecked but were later returned to service, the number certainly swells into the thousands. Most did not mysteriously vanish like the *Griffon.* In addition to the perils of storm-tossed seas, a number of circumstances claimed many hundreds of lake boats. Collisions, groundings, strands, fires, boiler explosions, and capsizing all contributed to the demise of ships, often with breath-taking loss of life. But above all, the sinister wrath of the storms that brew over the Great Lakes has challenged and defeated some of the staunchest vessels ever constructed in the shipyards of port cities along the U.S. and Canadian lakeshores.

Shipbuilding here evolved along with shipping worldwide: sail gave way to steam; wood gave way to iron and then to steel construction. Notwithstanding even the latest technologies in ship construction, many lake boats were susceptible to calamity in the face of the heavy weather so common on the Great Lakes. All styles of ships, all materials of construction, all kinetics of propulsion, have found the lake bottoms over the centuries since the *Griffon.*

Perhaps it is hard to understand why so many ships went down, in light of the very nature of where they occurred—in lakes. The notion of shipwrecks may conjure the wild vastness of oceans where hurricanes form and whales frolic, not the placid fresh water of lakes. But once you have eyed the enormous expanse of fresh water that comprises the Great Lakes—the largest body of fresh water in the world—the prevalence of wrecks ceases to surprise. When you have seen the lakes and heard the winds howl, you can come to understand.

On June 26, 1959, the St. Lawrence Seaway officially opened. U.S. president Dwight D. Eisenhower and Her Majesty Queen Elizabeth II presided over the ceremonies. Through dredged waterways and a series of locks and canals linking the Great Lakes to the Gulf of St. Lawrence and the Atlantic Ocean, oceangoing ships from across the globe were accorded access to the robust economies of the United States and Canada as never before. This trade remains vibrant today. But the ease of navigating the St. Lawrence River after that day in 1959 mustn't be considered the start of sailing the river for commercial gain, for the practice was born nearly a century before. In two of the opening chapters of this book, I write about two early lake boats that traveled and traded extensively in the ocean trades, utilizing the St. Lawrence River in a wilder era.

The purpose of this book is to detail the fascinating stories of a few of the many ships that sailed the Great Lakes, mostly in the late nineteenth and early twentieth centuries. Some of the accounts in this book have been related elsewhere and by others. In those cases, I have sought to add to the record, to provide more details or background story, and to expand upon the legacies of these ships and peoples and disasters. I researched and wrote these pieces over many years, without the idea that they would ever come together in a book. As a result, readers may begin anywhere in the book, guided by their own interests.

This book is not merely a study of shipwrecks, compelling though the subject is. In a couple of instances I cover only the launchings and entrance into service of two iconic lake boats, the *Eastland* and the *Augustus B. Wolvin*, that would later meet contrasting fates. Of the horrific nightmare that is the *Eastland*, there is much written. A sleek and surly passenger boat, the *Eastland* suffered the greatest disaster ever to befall a ship in the history of the Great Lakes when, laden with excursionists and set to depart her dock on the Chicago River, she capsized on July 24, 1915. Most of the passengers were employees of the Western Electric Company aboard for the company's annual outing, and first-generation immigrants from Europe. Eight hundred thirty-five of them drowned that nightmare morning, mere feet away from the safety of the dock. Even at the ship's launch, which I cover here, there were dark shadows of foreboding.

The *Wolvin*'s inauguration was the antithesis. It was a prototype, a trend setter, a marvel and monstrosity that captivated the interest of shippers and shipbuilders throughout the Great Lakes communities when it launched. It also caught the eyes: the *Wolvin* sported a most unusual yellow hull.

Although sailing the Great Lakes remained a dangerous business, many technological and regulatory changes helped to make shipping safer during the decades covered here. Two of the most important were the invention of the radio and the adoption of the load line. In 1909, Guglielmo Marconi shared the Nobel Prize in Physics with Karl Ferdinand Braun "in recognition of their contributions to wireless telegraphy." Marconi was certainly no seaman. Yet his passion for developing and improving wireless messaging, or what the world would come to refer to as radio, was steeped in the hopes of establishing a medium for communications between ships at sea and between ships and land-based stations. Such communications would be a safety feature he knew could save countless lives and improve information circulation as well. It could theoretically revolutionize communications, and as it did, it was championed around the world. Inexorably, radio would make its way to the Great Lakes, where it met a range of responses from eager to lukewarm to negative. The push for wireless use on the ships of the Great Lakes came at a time when the most effective means of communicating with a ship and land was a message ferried by a carrier pigeon. The cautious implementation of the use of radios on the ships of the Great Lakes is taken up herein.

So too is another European import that gained traction painfully slowly on the Great Lakes, at least in ships of the American fleets: the load line. Englishman Samuel Plimsoll gave his name to a load line mark that became compulsory for British ships in 1876. Plimsoll, an egalitarian and rabble rouser, had fought for the implementation of a safe load line since being elected to Parliament in 1867. He had waged his war against the callous practice of overloading, then over-insuring, ships sent to sea. Profitability trumped safety, as these overloaded ships were more likely to sink. Plimsoll called for requiring ships to bear a line indicating how heavy a load they could safely carry. Plimsoll's name is still attached to the hull marking to this day. However, the ships of the American fleets on the Great Lakes wouldn't bear load lines until the United States was wrestling free from the weight of the Great Depression.

The inclusion of the *Red, White & Blue* warrants explanation. This remarkable nineteenth-century lake boat sailed into—and through—a panoply of circumstances. Although its storied career ended on a shoal in Green Bay of Lake Michigan, it exemplified the durability often exhibited by vessels built on the Great Lakes. Fresh water, and the absence of corrosive salt water, allowed the *Red, White & Blue* to enjoy a career—checkered though it was—as lengthy as some recently scrapped 730-foot steel-hulled modern freighters. Its career encompassed all that makes Great Lakes maritime history rich, so I tell its story here.

I point out the merger of essay and historical perspectives with a few chapters in this book. The story of Philo Parsons—the man and the boat—reveals my lifelong tie to the *Milwaukee Clipper* and the astounding Welland Canal.

Some years back, seeking the tomb of former Detroit mayor Coleman A. Young in Detroit's historic Elmwood Cemetery, I unwittingly discovered Philo Parsons's grave. This chance encounter set the account offered here in motion. The connection to the grave of a long-forgotten prosperous Detroiter and his namesake vessel is enriched by the historical context of the ship *Philo Parsons.* It was the only vessel that fell to Confederate pirates on the Great Lakes during the American Civil War.

As a teen in 1970, I was able to take a trip across Lake Michigan on the doughty *Clipper* in its final year of operation. The ship, still with us today as a national historic landmark, is an extraordinary relic by any measure. A deeper look into this floating time capsule on Muskegon Lake reveals that it can be linked to the first iron-built ship on the Great Lakes and to the world's only nuclear-powered passenger and package freighter ever built, the *Savannah*, afloat today in Baltimore harbor.

Readers may be aware of the gales of November that for time immemorial have destroyed ships and claimed horrifying numbers of lives on the Lakes. They may be familiar with any number of iconic lighthouses that dot the shorelines or may have contemplated any number of rapturous sunsets or sunrises over the vast waters. To many, however, the Welland Canal is a mystery. Nevertheless, it is a crucial piece of the area's infrastructure and the stories I tell here. When the *City of Green Bay* and the *Mary L. Higgie* set out on their respective ocean adventures, they had to make a transit through that period's iteration of this waterway. Modern freighters as well as saltwater ships visiting and trading on the Great Lakes must do so via today's aging but established Welland Canal and its amazing locks. An essay on the Welland Canal concludes this book.

It is possible to reconnoiter with historic Great Lakes vessels at various port cities along the sinuous coastlines. Museum ships are popular attractions. In an array of maritime museums scattered among the Great Lakes' communities, artifacts from earlier times are on display. Many casualties of the Great Lakes, invisible beneath the surface of the waters, are destinations for divers of varying levels of skill. A surprising number of vessels that foundered and went missing are still missing to this day, despite decades of searching and improved technology to find them. This serves as further testament to the wonder and breadth, the grandeur and depths, of these unparalleled bodies of water.

Nearly all of the vessels covered in these pages that met with grief are but fusty memories. But there are exceptions beyond the still-stunning *Clipper.* On display at a visitor center of the Apostle Islands National Lakeshore is the capstan cover of the *Emily P. Weed*, a gorgeous artifact. The cabin built from her hatch covers when she wrecked as the *Sevona* remains, and is on the register of historic places for the state of Wisconsin. The nameboard from the *Arcadia* was once on display at the visitor center of the Sleeping Bear Dunes National Lakeshore, and is believed to be in the collections of the National Park Service. The tugboat *Richard Fitzgerald* is still with us as the Great Lakes Towing Company's venerable *Superior.* For how much longer is uncertain, however. In the late summer of 2020, as I wrote this, it was towed to Cleveland, the Great Lakes Towing Company's home port, along with two aged sister ships, for inspection and evaluation.

The enormity and expanse of the Great Lakes may be read as a capacity of history these waters have floated. Their vastness ensures that stories will always be told. That memories can fade but never die. In the wake of one of the mammoth, unaesthetic, thousand-foot freighters plying the Great Lakes today, the specter of the *Griffon* endures.

Acknowledgments

The stories that comprise this book span and encompass many years. The research and writing were oft interrupted, sometimes lying fallow for years. I have reopened an envelope containing a letter postmarked from Bowling Green, Ohio, dated September 2, 1976. The envelope is crisp, a bit time-faded and slightly marred. The message from the letter writer concerns an inquiry I had sent to him about a vessel described in this book, the sandsucker *Kelley Island.* At the time of our correspondence the research facility he oversaw was known as the Northwest Ohio–Great Lakes Research Center. Today, the database is known as the Historical Collections of the Great Lakes at Bowling Green State University. The letter was signed by the then-director of the center, Richard J. Wright.

Dr. Wright has been gone since 1986. Posthumously alluding to his contribution to this book must allow for the recognition of his successors, for they too have aided me along the path. The Center at Bowling Green State University later became the Institute for Great Lakes Research. Around this period, my correspondence with Robert W. Graham commenced. Over the years he supplied me with information and data vital to this work. Moreover, current archivist Mark Sprang has been invaluable in making this book happen. With his diligence and cheerful assistance, he rolls out a welcome mat every time I knock on his door.

I have not personally met any of the aforementioned. I have met Suzette J. Lopez, firekeeper of the unparalleled Marine Historical Collection of the Milwaukee Public Library. Suzette has, over the years, fed me information, data, documents, and photo images. Her encouragement, along with her caretaking of Great Lakes maritime history housed in the library, is vital to telling these stories. My gratitude and appreciation for Suzette are deep.

I am indebted to Steve Harold, former director of the Manistee (Michigan) County Historical Museum. We have been friendly for decades, and Steve was instrumental in providing material for the *Arcadia* chapter.

I am thankful for the assistance of Jay Bascom. Jay edits the *Scanner*, the superb journal of the Toronto Marine Historical Society. Jay's standing in the realm of Great Lakes maritime historians is unsurpassed on either side of the U.S.–Canada border.

I am grateful for the support of Nancy Schneider, editor of *Inland Seas*, the fine quarterly journal of the National Museum of the Great Lakes at Toledo, Ohio. Thanks too to Stephen Haynes of the Wisconsin Marine Historical Society. A boost of thanks to John Buellesbach. Thanks for insights and pointers from Wayne Niebrowski. Ann Matteson and Mark Bowden of the Detroit Public Library have assisted in getting this book to print.

From Chicago, my nephew Matthew Perley smoothed the rough edges and majestically polished the bibliography and source notes. His efforts and sanguine encouragement in coaxing this project over the finish line were unwavering. To him and all the aforementioned, a profound appreciation and artesian thanks.

Havana, California, City of Green Bay, Linked in Coincidence

The year before the *City of Green Bay* arrived on the shipping scene, in 1872, the *Havana*, a 306-ton schooner built at Oswego, New York, a moderate-size fore-and-aft schooner, entered the Great Lakes bulk commodities trade. It's unclear what festivities surrounded her launch and anticipated entrance to service. We do have information on the former.

When Lambert Nau's *City of Green Bay* completed fit-out at her namesake Wisconsin city on August 25, 1872, it was one month and one day after her launch. Nau invited several cronies, all prominent Green Bay residents, aboard for the maiden voyage of his fine new schooner. It was little more than a glorified harbor cruise as the boat was sailed due north on Green Bay to Pensaukee, Wisconsin, roughly eighteen miles distant. There, Nau and guests disembarked the ship as her first payload of lumber was brought aboard, destined for Chicago. A correspondent for the *Green Bay Gazette* had also been aboard. In reporting how neatly fitted and magnificent the vessel was, he underscored the maiden voyage of the *City of Green Bay* poignantly and closed his brief column, "Long may she sail."

In 1873 the Canadian propeller *California* entered service. The trio would then be linked to the calendar, successive years from one another not only in the chronological timetable of their origins, but in shared experiences their futures would hold. When the *California*, resplendent from the builders in Hamilton, Ontario, arrived at Chicago on her maiden voyage on August 11, 1873, newspapers published accolades.

The 179-foot long, 580-net-ton *California* was one of eleven boats operated by the Lake & River Steamship Line between Montreal and Chicago. In addition to the Lake & River Line, the Merchants Line operated nine steamers between Canadian ports and Chicago. In a vibrantly colorful era with a plethora of passenger steamers crossing and running the length of Lake Michigan, the *California* joined well over one hundred vessels in the passenger and package freight trade. Outside Canadian origins, they smoked into Chicago from Buffalo and Ogdensburg, New York; Port Huron, Michigan; Lake Superior ports; and all port cities on Lake Michigan. Like most of them, the *California* would carry some bulk cargoes, usually related to the food chain; wheat, grain, corn, and barreled products and sundries. along with a complement of passengers.

The year 1874 would broach the *City of Green Bay*'s dramatic history. In the summer she rubbed the schooner *Minnie Slauson* at Chicago and sustained minor damage. In November she called on Chicago less her mizzen boom and sail, which had been carried away in a gale.

For the *California*, an auspicious event marked her early years of service. On June 14, 1875, she arrived at Duluth, Minnesota, with, besides passengers and other things, railroad iron loaded at Montreal. Significantly, the *California* had reached Montreal from Pictou, Nova Scotia. Although the *California* loaded railroad iron at Montreal, she was given credit for being the first vessel ever to reach Duluth from a salt water port, as her voyage began at Pictou, Nova Scotia.

Pomp and pageantry had marked the *California*'s departure from Pictou on Victoria Day, May 25, in honor of Queen Victoria's birthday.[1] With pennants and flags fluttering aloft and cannons booming ashore, the send-off was worthy of royalty. The proud *California* moved up the Gulf of St. Lawrence under the command of Scottish Captain J. W. Leslie, a man portrayed in the historical record as an engaging conversationalist. Having loaded the railroad iron at Montreal, Leslie guided the steamboat up the St. Lawrence River, through Lake Ontario, the Welland Canal, and Lake Erie. At Detroit, Captain Burton Atkins of Duluth joined the *California* as a pilot. On Lake Superior the *California* had soon overtaken the

1. Canada was then still a part of Great Britain.

steamers *Asia* and *Europe*, which had departed Montreal well before her. She arrived at Duluth several hours before both of them, and with his Scottish brogue Leslie was only too happy to bend the ears of all listeners about his greyhound flyer, fresh from Nova Scotia.

In 1877, the *City of Green Bay* had fallen into the hands of C. W. Elphicke. The Chicago-based Elphicke was ubiquitous in the shipping industry of the period, wearing the hats of investor, agent, and insurer of lake boats. It was a noteworthy time for specific shipping interests on the Great Lakes, as economic opportunities beckoned from abroad. Domestically, the United States was still shaking off the effects of the Panic of 1873, and the commodity in demand was wood. A strong demand in some European cities for hard- and softwood harvested from the Great Lakes states captured the attention of Elphicke and others. In managing the *City of Green Bay*, Elphicke was advantageously positioned to send the schooner abroad, profitably laden with lumber.

Via the Welland Canal and the St. Lawrence River, the same route taken by the *California*, the *City of Green Bay* was sent abroad with a lumber cargo in her hold in the late spring of 1877. She arrived at Dundee, Scotland, in June. Unloaded of her lumber, she had her hold filled with coal, slated for a delivery at Montreal. This return cargo would underscore a problem on the transatlantic voyages lake boats would embark upon. Lake port cities and the shipping concerns engaged in this cross-ocean trade didn't need European coal. Domestic resources were plentiful and much less expensive to obtain.

When the *City of Green Bay* was set to sail from Montreal it was Elphicke's decision, as nearly as can be determined, to send the schooner back to the Atlantic Ocean. There the ship headed south. Into the vastness of the Atlantic, shaking off the ocean spray, the schooner from the Great Lakes and her people—utterly unknown—were taking a journey to far-flung destinations. As the *City of Green Bay* sailed south, crossing the equator into the South Atlantic and the Southern Hemisphere, it seems reasonable that her crewmembers, sailors of the Great Lakes, were setting eyes at night for their first time on southern constellations. Her travels and trading in the South American continent and interior may very well have been the first for a lake boat.

The miscellany of her cargo hold may never be detailed. She docked at Buenos Aires, Argentina, then up the Parana River. Likely at Paso de la Patrina, where the Parana branches with the Paraguay River, she made her way to the Paraguayan capital city of Asuncion, hundreds of miles from Buenos Aires and the Atlantic

Ocean. We can only guess at the hull color of the *City of Green Bay*, but it is certain that upon her arrival at Asuncion the port city was bright with similar sailing craft of various shades and hues. Upon those transom sterns were lettered the names of ships likely as colorful as their distant ports of hail. Doubtless the crew of the vagabond Great Lakes schooner, so far from home, ate dishes exotic to them; they may have traced the Southern Cross with a finger in the cobalt sky.

When the *City of Green Bay* worked her way back to the Atlantic, she was off for Rio De Janeiro. Maybe sailors from the Great Lakes states were making notes about the similarities and disparities of South American cities they had only known from scholastic studies. The schooner loaded assorted merchandise at Rio and sailed for Liverpool, England, setting the stage for drama. While off the Spanish coast, the boat was beset by four days of brutal weather. She lost her bowsprit and a topmast. Her canvas was shredded, hanging worthlessly in strings the color of mozzarella. Her crewmembers were exhausted, and as they pondered abandoning the *City of Green Bay*, they were sighted by an unnamed brigantine and taken under tow to Lisbon, Portugal.

Repaired at Lisbon, the vagabond schooner set sail across the Atlantic. Storms continued to flail away at her. Late in 1879, when she arrived at Trinidad in the West Indies, pummeled along the way by the ocean, inspectors there threatened to condemn her.

News of the situation of the *City of Green Bay* reached Chicago somehow. Captain J. B. Hall, familiar with the boat, sprang into action to save the argosy. Hall went to Trinidad, and for a nominal sum purchased the bruised vessel and refitted her. Early in 1880 Hall was sailing the *City of Green Bay* and trading between New Orleans and New England ports. It is reasonable to think the schooner loaded staples such as coffee, sugar, and molasses at New Orleans. It isn't clear how many trips the ship made in this endeavor, but certainly not many. Hall's burning desire was to bring the *City of Green Bay* back to the Great Lakes, her home and his. On July 9, 1880, Hall achieved his goal. The *City of Green Bay* tied up to a dock at Chicago that day, and the tales of the wandering and victimized lake boat that sailed so far from home were written in the *Chicago Inter-Ocean.*

The construction of the *Havana*, *City of Green Bay*, and *California* in successive years in the early 1870s would be shadowed by incidents and encumbrances befalling each on consecutive years in the 1880s. For all three, the episodes would occur on Lake Huron.

Early Saturday morning, May 19, 1883, cloaked in fog near Thunder Bay Island on

Lake Huron, under command of Captain Foster, the *City of Green Bay* ran aground.[2] Foster would leave an impression on the lifesavers, when the report did make print, as a rather irascible, blustery sort. Stranding some five hundred yards out, the schooner was at first invisible to those ashore. A northeast wind whisked the fog away, and as it lifted, the crew of the station could make out the vague outline of the grounded schooner and set out to her. When they arrived and offered to remove the schooner's crew, the inhospitable Foster refused the gesture. Concluding that the ship and crew were in no imminent danger, the lifesavers concluded they might as well go back to the station and make breakfast.

The wind increased and a sea began to build along the shore at Thunder Bay Island and the marooned *City of Green Bay.* At ten in the morning the lifesavers rowed back out to the schooner. Foster was by now agitated, asking to be taken to Alpena, Michigan, where a tug could be procured. The station keeper offered to take Foster and deliver him to Alpena if he would in turn allow the ship's crew to be removed. Foster balked, asking for transfer to nearer Sugar Island, where he could persuade a fisherman to take him to Alpena. The keeper delivered Foster to Sugar Island and pleaded once more with him to allow the lifesavers to bring the schooner's crew ashore. The cranky Foster finally acquiesced, telling him to "do as he pleased with the matter." It isn't clear why Foster was reluctant to have his crewmembers removed. The ship was stuck fast and it was pointless to have them remain onboard. Perhaps the voice of authority was speaking in a time of humiliation with his ship on the beach. The lifesavers did as they pleased, removing six anxious people from the stricken boat in a heavy, pelting rainstorm. Seesawing on her perch with six feet of water in her hold, the *City of Green Bay* "reared and plunged like a wild horse," in the keeper's words.

In a comic pair of events the next day, the wind shifted back to the west, blowing the sea out. The lifesavers took the crew back to the grounded vessel. When the wind shifted to the northeast, the lifesavers rowed back out and removed the crew once again.

On Monday the 21st, the big tug *Martin Swain* arrived with steam pumps. Water in the *City of Green Bay*'s hold now stood at nine feet deep. In miserable weather, 250 tons of coal was lightered over the side and she was refloated. The next morning the boat and the brooding Captain Foster were on their way to drydock.

2. No first name was recorded for Captain Foster in either the Lifesaving Service's subsequent report or newspaper account.

In a similar atmospheric theater, on the same lake a little over a year later, June 9, 1884, the *California* was groping through a thick chowder of fog. There were fourteen passengers along with her crew of twenty-one, as she was bound for her dock at Montreal with a cargo of corn. The *California* ran aground on a reef two miles north of the Sand Beach Life Saving Station.[3] After the fog lifted, the lifesavers, as was the case for the *City of Green Bay* the year before, started to see the outline of a ship clearly in distress. There was no resistance in this episode, and the crew and passengers of the *California* were removed.

The *California*'s hold flooded, immersing her cargo, perhaps giving the boat the appearance of a gigantic open can of whole kernel water-packed corn. The dense slurry clogged pumps employed to clear the ship of water. For three days the crew of the ship, aided by surfmen from the lifesaving station, shoveled corn out of freight doors and openings.

At last, on the evening of June 13, the countless bushels of corn jettisoned from the steamer and the sedulous pumps achieved their goal and the *California* floated free. She was towed into Sand Beach harbor, where a diver made a temporary patch on her hull, enabling the longer trip to drydock.

Twenty-eight miles south of Sand Beach, in lower Michigan's "thumb" region, near the town of Forester, the *Havana* found the beach. In the wee hours of August 4, 1885, bound for Cleveland from Marquette, Michigan, with iron ore, it was driven ashore during a summer gale. When the lifesavers from the Sand Beach station arrived on the scene that afternoon, they were apoplectic at the oddity they confronted: local children were patrolling the *Havana*'s deck. How else but to picture these kids, tatterdemalions with hands on hips, staring back at the lifesavers and asking what had taken them so long to get there. They *could* answer the lifesavers' questions about the crewmembers of the beached schooner, however: they had already gone ahead to the town of Forester to seek assistance.

The stranded *Havana* was a sight. Water sloshed around in her cargo of iron ore. Her sails were streams of crepe paper, and booms were broken like pretzel sticks. Crewmen from the *Havana* and three men from the lifesaving station worked for two days shoveling her ore cargo over the side. The tug *Mocking Bird* and a lighter arrived with steam pumps to relieve the schooner of the water in her hold. When the wind picked up on August 6 and the *Havana* began rocking on her perch on the beach, she was permitted to refill with water and settle to prevent her from

3. Sand Beach is today known as Harbor Beach.

pounding heavily and sustaining even more damage. Pumped out again the next day, the *Havana* was towed to Port Huron for what promised to be costly repairs.

The trio's brushes with potentially destructive incidents in consecutive years on Lake Huron would be overlooked by the opening days of October 1887. The curtain was going up on their final act, a denouement orchestrated by a Lake Michigan Ride of the Valkyrie. Saturday evening, October 1, the *California* was at Chicago, taking on a load of twenty thousand bushels of corn and 594 barrels of pork. When it set sail that night, a fresh northwest wind rose. As the wind gained force and began raking the lake, the seas rose, setting the stage for the dramatics to come. With the wind howling like demons and devastating seas building through Sunday the second, the *California* was in for a ride. The *City of Green Bay* and the *Havana*, both laden with iron ore from Escanaba, Michigan, and bound for St. Joseph, Michigan, would battle through that wretched Sunday.

When daylight came Monday morning, October 3, the breadth of Lake Michigan was wracked with violent seas and hurricane west winds. Up and down the eastern shore of the lake, harbors burgeoned with sheltered craft. At the Manitous, fourteen identified and a number of unnamed vessels were lying at anchor as the storm raged. Early Monday morning, the *City of Green Bay* was stranded just south of the South Haven, Michigan, piers. Further south, the *Havana* suffered the same fate, off the entrance to St. Joseph harbor. When the vessels grounded, that ended the earlier similarities—the same port of departure, same cargo, same destination. There was stark contrast in the final chapters in the histories of the *City of Green Bay* and the *Havana*: one of frightful ineptness, the other of enormous courage.

The *City of Green Bay* struck broadside to the beach, pounding heavily until she came within roughly 180 yards of the beach. Massive seas rolled completely over her, driving her crew into the rigging of her foremast. When discovered by the lifesavers from the South Haven station in her desperate plight, the luckless people of the *City of Green Bay* were in the hands of bumbling Captain Barney Cross, whose miscues would prove fatal.

Failing to secure the services of a tug to tow the station's lifeboat out to the stricken schooner, Cross had the breeches buoy apparatus carted to the beach by a team of horses. In his haste, he neglected to include the service's surfboat. Shot from the beach by Lyle gun, two lines of No. 7 hawser parted before reaching the *City of Green Bay.* A miniature cannon-like device, the Lyle gun was developed to shoot a potential lifeline to stricken or shipwrecked vessels near shore. Fixing a line to the ship and shore would impart stability to implement the evacuation of crew and passengers with the breeches buoy. Now realizing his gaffe in not bringing the surfboat, Cross sent two surfmen at once to the station for it. He also overlooked bringing to the scene the heavier No. 9 hawser. Clinging to the schooner's rigging and suffering from exposure, the crewmembers held on as Cross mounted a horse and galloped off to meet the surfboat.

Precious time was wasted—forty-five minutes—before one of the surfmen arrived with the No. 9 line. A shot reached the *City of Green Bay* between the fore and mainmast, where it was quickly grabbed by two sailors. They had barely retrieved the line when the mainmast collapsed. With the mizzenmast already lost over the side, the sailors retreated from their foremast perch, fearing it too would topple. As the crew was being inundated by seas thundering over the hulk of the schooner, the line shot out to them became a casualty of the turmoil and was hopelessly fouled.

When Cross arrived and the surfboat was launched, the rescue effort was further encumbered by floating debris and wreckage, as the *City of Green Bay* was rapidly breaking up. One by one, the crewmembers of the schooner dropped into the raging water, merely a short distance from the surfboat that miserable morning, and only one, sailor Adelbert Slater, would survive. Slater, clinging to a piece of the *City of Green Bay*'s deck, tumbled within arm's length of the surfboat and pulled to safety. The *City of Green Bay*'s Captain P. W. Costello's lifeless body was plucked from the water and efforts to resuscitate him proved futile. Besides Captain Costello, five others lost their lives that horrid morning off South Haven—mate Frank Wood, cook Patrick O'Leary, and seamen Tom Hoitman and Henry Barkett. Adding injury to insult, Cross was pitched from the surfboat into the raging water. He was continually bludgeoned by pieces of wreckage and submerged by huge breakers. As the surfboat drew near to rescue him, the stern post struck him in the side, fracturing several of his ribs.

The errors committed by Cross in the desultory rescue attempt of the *City of Green Bay* resulted in his discharge from the United States Life-Saving Service. Although his record as a surfman at the Muskegon Station had been impeccable, his promotion to captain at South Haven left much to be desired. "A good soldier does not always make a good captain" was how it was worded in the *United States Life-Saving Service Annual Report.* It was Cross's first serious shipwreck since assuming command of the South Haven Station, and his last. "He completely lost his head and committed a succession of blunders which turned an easy prospective victory into a disastrous defeat and cost the lives of six men," the report concluded.

Charles Mollhagen and engineer August Kuehn, owners of the fish tug *Hannah Sullivan*, would earn them the highest award presented by the Life-Saving Service, the gold medal, for their heroics in the rescue of the *Havana*'s survivors. As the battered *Havana* neared the beach, the mountains of water she had battled finally overwhelmed her. She foundered, leaving only her masts protruding above the rampaging lake surface. The *Havana*'s crew of seven had taken to her main- and foremasts, clinging to life as the *City of Green Bay*'s ill-fated crew had. When the mainmast snapped and fell into the water, three of her men were pitched to their deaths, including Captain John Curran. Fearful the foremast was also likely to be snapped from the submerged deck of the sunken schooner, Mollhagen and Kuehn momentarily pondered the grim situation. There was no guarantee the *Hannah Sullivan* could clear the sandbar near the channel mouth, where seas were breaking in spectacular fashion. What they did know, however, was that the remaining crewmen holding on to a fragile stick of mast left remaining from the *Havana* would soon perish without aid. Despite the life-threatening danger, seven other men volunteered to assist Mollhagen and Kuehn, and the gallant *Hannah Sullivan* chugged away.

Outside the piers, the little fish tug burrowed into the seas that swept her from stem to stern. Like a cork, she popped out of each horrifying onslaught and, miraculously, was soon maneuvering near the site of the sunken *Havana*. In a sensational feat that would later consecrate the presentation of a gold medal, the four remaining crewmen of the schooner were taken aboard the *Hannah Sullivan*. As the *Hannah Sullivan* rolled and pitched, defying calamity, Mollhagen sailed the worthy fish tug back into the safety of St. Joseph harbor.

The *California*'s wild ride throughout Monday had brought her near the neck of Lake Michigan as dusk set in. Near the Straits of Mackinac, punishment the steamer had been subjected to was taking its toll. There was difficulty in getting the steamer to respond to the wheel, indicating some possible rudder damage. Water was rising in her hold as seams in her wooden hull yawned wider. The desperate condition so alarmed Captain John V. Trowell that he instructed passengers to don life preservers.

Maddeningly close to rounding the Straits of Mackinac and tucking into sheltered water, disaster struck the *California* shortly after midnight, October 4. Near St. Helena Island the vessel grounded. Huge waves boarded her, stripping away her deck gear and masts, hammering away at her cabins. Captain Trowell made the call to prepare the crew and passengers to abandon the imperiled ship. In the midst of the crisis, First Mate Peter Desbon and others from the *California*'s apparently impetuous crew—numbers and names not revealed—launched a lifeboat and hauled away from the stricken steamer. Desbon—a figure whose character and actions would be tarred as negligent by reports following the disaster published in the *Chicago Inter-Ocean*—left Captain Trowell in insuperable hardship. Without the capable assistance of crewmen responsible for orderly launch of lifeboats—and left with only one boat—Trowell's abilities to safely land the *California*'s people was mortally handicapped.

Trowell, a stewardess with the surname Blood, an engineer with the surname Ellis, a second engineer named Mills, a wheelsman, Owen Rourke, and a handful of unnamed crewmembers had managed to free the remaining lifeboat when the coup de grâce fell. The *California* turned turtle, her cabins collapsing as she rolled. For several hours the lifeboat and fortunate occupants tossed about in the waters of the Straits of Mackinac. It was reported that in addition to those in the lifeboat, two unidentified men from the ship clung to the gunwale of the lifeboat for a brief time. Whether they were not pulled aboard for lack of room in the boat or simply because no one in the lifeboat had the strength to pull them in isn't clear. The inescapable consequence was that they were lost, along with seven others.

The beach of Cecil Bay, between Mackinaw City and Waugoshance Point, was littered with wreckage by midday. The derelict hulk of the *California* was still afloat when the bodies of the victims reached shore. Seven of the nine who lost their lives came ashore in Cecil Bay with wreckage, including passengers Minnie Membery of Sackett's Harbor, New York, and Cornelius Connorton of Detroit, the only two passengers lost from the disaster.

As sailors and marine men absorbed the sad plight of the *California*, many asserted Desbon's dereliction of duty was a profoundly responsible factor. If Desbon had remained with Trowell and helped direct the abandonment of the steamer, they felt, the ship could have been evacuated with no loss of life.

It isn't clear what Cross and Desbon were doing with their lives some two weeks later when the last of the *City of Green Bay*'s crewmen, believed to be John Williams, was found on the beach near South Haven. It seems reasonable to think both men could be tormented by their roles—or lack thereof—in the grim aftermath of the horrors they witnessed.

A note in the ship's profile sheet from records at the fine archives held by Bowling Green State University at Ohio indicate that the *California*'s corn cargo was purchased by Detroit distiller Hiram Walker, presumably to cook into a sour mash to make whiskey. Relegated to the dim- lighted rowhouse of ignominious Great Lakes history, Desbon and Cross could only hope to meet one day at some lakefront saloon. No one would blame them for any amount of Hiram Walker's blend they consumed.

The *California* would resurface. Recovered and rebuilt by American Edward S. Pease, the rejuvenated steamboat was named after him in 1889. On November 24, 1904, the *Pease* was destroyed by fire at Collingwood, Ontario. Records indicate it was active as a barge into the 1920s.

The Immaculate Disappearance of the *Thomas Hume*

William Walsh was not being unreasonable when, in August 1870, he protested the $200 repair bill he was presented for the caulking job performed on his schooner, the *H. C. Albrecht*. The *Albrecht* was brand new, so when the boat sprang a leak shortly after entering service, it would warrant pique. If, however, Walsh had been worried that the dubious episode of an untimely leak on his proud new ship might prove a harbinger of things to come, he wouldn't be incorrect.

Built at Manitowoc, Wisconsin, the 209-ton *Albrecht* measured 131 feet six inches in overall length, a beam of slightly over twenty-six feet, drawing eight feet of water. Built chiefly for the Lake Michigan lumber trade, the ship occasionally loaded "wild" cargoes, such as early season grain to Georgian Bay ports and even rarer iron ore deliveries to Chicago from Escanaba, Michigan. Primarily a lumber schooner, the *Albrecht* rarely strayed from the Muskegon, Michigan, to Chicago route when she was in service on Lake Michigan.

Good fortune accompanied the *Albrecht* over the years, making the leaking hull in her initial season of operation aberrant. In the following years there were a number of destructive storms that swirled and agitated Lake Michigan that the *Albrecht* avoided. In fact, it seemed a natural order that the boat's gravitating for

Muskegon would eventually lead to the city being her home port, especially in view of the calamity she avoided by sheltering there in some of those heavy blows. Two examples stand out.

In late November 1879, the Canadian passenger steamer *Waubuno* was lost on Georgian Bay during a gale, resulting in staggering loss of life. The same storm pounded Lake Michigan, resulting in widespread damage to vessels the length of the lake. The *Albrecht* left Chicago just before the fury of the gale unleashed, managing to sail into the Muskegon harbor safely. Snug at a dock, she waited for the storm to subside.

A year later, in mid October 1880, the Goodrich line steamer *Alpena* foundered, claiming all hands during a monstrous combination of wind and seas on Lake Michigan. Damage was extensive. Again, the *Albrecht* was moored on Muskegon Lake, this time with twenty-one other schooners and three steam barges, and providence reigned over the sheltered Muskegon fleet.

Even when the *Albrecht* found herself in difficult passages on Lake Michigan, such as one arrival at Chicago late in the 1881 shipping season, this elicited poetry over concern from the marine news columnist of the *Chicago Inter-Ocean.* The *Albrecht,* along with the schooners *Levi Grant, Starlight, Robert Howlett,* and *Rouse Simmons,* had arrived following a rough trip in subfreezing temperatures in late November. The columnist described the quintet, heavily iced over, as "looking like moving icebergs."

Sold in 1883, the *Albrecht* was renamed *Thomas Hume,* in honor of the business partner of Charles H. Hackley of the Hackley–Hume Lumber Company, for whom she would commence working. Hackley arrived at Muskegon in the spring of 1856, a young and enterprising sort. Over the next quarter century his name would be synonymous with the city, remaining so today. He amassed a great fortune in the lumber business, and this legend was equal to his distribution of that wealth throughout the city. He became the city's great benefactor, and many of his gifts continue to flourish, most notably the Hackley Public Library, perhaps the brightest jewel in the city's crown.

Hackley rooted himself at Muskegon in the period of accelerated expansion of the lumbering era in Michigan. The great stands of white pine were falling in ever-increasing numbers from logging camps throughout the interior or the state. The year after Hackley arrived, the state legislature appropriated $50,000 for improvements on the Muskegon River and at the junction of Muskegon Lake, to open a broader, deeper flow over the river flats. Already there were fifteen sawmills on Muskegon Lake; the number would grow exponentially, and the influx of state spending on the venture was viewed as viable and healthy to all concerns.

As the skilled, nimble rivermen rode logs downriver from the lumber camps and into Muskegon Lake, the sheer number of logs marked and destined for individual sawmills set off a whole new series of issues for mill operators. Separating a company's logs into rafts to be towed to their respective mills was an elephantine challenge.

Enter the Muskegon Booming Company. Organized in 1864, Muskegon Booming Company's function was culling logs and dispatching them to sorting pens for the individual lumber companies. Once corralled, the logs could be fixed in rafts and towed to their designated company mills. The booming company had a fleet of several tugs employed in this venture, and the pen area stretched along the south shore of Muskegon Lake from the river to roughly the area at the foot of Ottawa Street. Tugs had rich names: *Pony, Boss, Comet, Winnie Mees, Ira O. Smith,* and *Third Michigan.*

According to a report, the *Comet, Ira O. Smith,* and *Third Michigan* were each equipped with a stout pump and a thousand feet of hose, doubling their role as nascent fireboats. The report read, "As the tugs burn slabs, sparks often set fire to sawdust around the lake and protection for vessels was necessary."

Numerous cities and towns along rivers feeding the lakes of Michigan and Wisconsin and ultimately Lake Michigan (and in some cases, Lake Huron) would be notable in the lumbering era on the Great Lakes. None would exceed the prolific output of Muskegon. The city would establish the benchmark. By the 1880s, Muskegon had forty-seven sawmills operating on Muskegon Lake, twenty-five of which were on the south shore of the lake. The mills and shingle works created a bevy of wealthy owners. Mills were frequently sold or reorganized, often changing hands in partnerships that evolved, fell apart, and redeveloped. As with other boomtowns of the Gilded Age, the laborers to carry out the work were far more numerous than the wealthy. It was backbreaking, arduous work that demanded hard play when laborers were free of its manacles. Saloons were plentiful, and gambling opportunities abundant to stretch or collapse your pocket of hard-earned cash. There were places to go whoring, if a man was up to it after an eleven-hour day.

The annual numbers of board feet of lumber shipped from Muskegon in the 1880s were staggering. Not in a single season did the total fall short of 426 million board feet, reaching a highwater mark of 685 million in 1884. The average for the decade was 519 million board feet per season.

The tugs of the Muskegon Booming Company being equipped to battle fires amid the threat posed by the combustible piles of sawdust illustrates one peril of the by-product of sawmills. In the halcyon days of lumbering in the 1880s, an essay by Frederick W. True was published, and although the subject matter was the state of fisheries, there was allusion to sawmills on Green Bay, and the water quality illuminated by the report provides a sobering view, as it was "not unusual for a vessel to meet portions of the mass of sawdust twenty or thirty miles from Menominee, and the water at the entrance of the bay is often covered with it. It is said to have accumulated at the mouth of the river, forming masses in some places eight feet deep." Incontestably, the ring of sawdust encircling Muskegon Lake would have been similar, a wheat-colored mass thick as porridge, creeping away from the lakeshore like blonde ice forming.

On Thursday May 21, 1891, the *Hume* was at Chicago, having divested herself of her latest load. The lumber era was starting its precipitous decline at the time, but the *Hume* and many others were holding their own, as was her nearby fleet sister, *Simmons*, which was still unloading. There was a northerly wind, brisk enough to kick up whitecaps on Lake Michigan. That evening, the *Hume* and *Simmons* left Chicago, bound once again for Muskegon to repeat the ritual. They made good progress for the first two hours, sailing gingerly into the slop of seas the wind created. A change of wind direction to the southwest, accompanied by heavy squalls and thunderstorms, altered things considerably. After laboring in the building seas for some time, the *Simmons* turned about and headed back to Chicago. The *Hume* maintained her course for Muskegon.

The *Simmons* was held in Chicago until late in the day on Friday. When she arrived at the Hackley–Hume dock in Muskegon, her captain expressed his surprise that the *Hume* had not called on the dock ahead of him. Reloaded, the *Simmons* returned to Chicago. After docking at her slip near Twenty-Second Street on the Chicago River, her captain roamed the lumber yards, inquiring and being inquired of about the whereabouts of the *Hume.* Although the location of the *Hume* was unknown, no immediate concern was expressed, as the life of a lake schooner was often fraught with delays.

A week after the *Hume* sailed, with still no tidings of her disposition, concerns were grave at the offices of the Hackley–Hume Lumber Company. So grave, in fact, that Hackley believed the *Hume* to be lost, and offered the following statement to a reporter from the Muskegon *Chronicle* reporter: "We don't care for the boat. It's the loss of the captain and the men that makes it sad. The captain has been in our employ for twelve years, was a reliable man and every inch a sailor."

The captain Hackley was referring to was Chicagoan Harry Albrightson. The Seaman's Union was able to identify two of the *Hume*'s sailors believed to be lost with Captain Albrightson, Oscar and Charles Anderson. Curiously, no sign of the *Hume* was reported and no evidence of her demise on Lake Michigan was found. No flotsam or wreckage or yawl, nothing that could have floated free from her cabins and been identified.

On the morning of May 30, the Hackley–Hume Lumber Company dispatched the tug *Sill* to scour Lake Michigan along the route the *Hume* would have traveled. Piloting the *Sill* was Captain Christian, while Captain Seth Lee served as lookout. The *Sill* meticulously searched the head of the lake from St. Joseph to Michigan City, Indiana, finding not even a warm clue.

In Muskegon, Hackley, while lamenting the loss of the *Hume*, defended the sterling safety record the vessels of the Hackley–Hume fleet enjoyed. "In the nineteen years we have been running our own vessels, this is our first serious accident," Hackley said. "We have never had a schooner go on the beach. All of our vessels were kept in first class condition and the captains always had instructions to get whatever they considered necessary for the security of the vessels and crew without asking for special permission. The *Hume* had two thousand dollars spent on her in repairs last winter. She carried a first class lifeboat and everything to insure safety for the crew in case of accident."

Hackley wasn't merely paying lip service. No mention of the *Hume* can be found in life-saving service reports, where extracting vessels from beaches was routine. Up to the time of the *Hume*'s loss, only once was his namesake vessel, the schooner *C. H. Hackley*, in need of lifesavers' assistance. That occurred on August 26, 1880, off Kenosha, Wisconsin, when the *Hackley*'s windlass was disabled. True to his word, Hackley–Hume vessels never found the beach.

The bizarre circumstance of no wreckage afloat on Lake Michigan perplexed the greatest marine minds. Collisions invariably leave some trace in the way of wreckage. Had a vessel cut through the *Hume* with such violence, the perpetrator would most certainly have sustained some damage that would have been visible, but no such case was reported. Two prevailing schools of thought encamped around the *Hume*'s mysterious disappearance. One was the collision theory, espoused not only by Lee and many others but by Hackley as well. In promoting the collision theory,

Lee took umbrage with the suggestion that no lake captain would deliberately leave the scene of a collision, having run down another boat. "I have sailed these lakes for forty years and I know of several cases," Lee hooted. "The fine schooner *Magellan* was one of them. If the officers of some steamers see a big loss to pay for, you bet they keep mum."

A more sensible explanation for the *Hume*'s disappearance was the sudden squalls raking the lake that forced the *Simmons* to return to Chicago while the *Hume* sailed on in a voyage she would never complete. In recorded histories of the Great Lakes, squalls have left a grim legacy, their very nature as diverse as the vessels they have claimed.

In June 1872, the schooner *Jamaica* was on Lake Huron only a few miles from shore with her sails set in a dead calm. She was struck by a sudden squall and instantly capsized, claiming the life of her female cook. The schooner *Hunter Savidge* was doomed by a squall under identical circumstances in August 1899 on the same lake with fatal results.

Squalls weren't limited to striking like a viper only on breezeless days. The loss of the 385-ton schooner *C. G. Breed*, a vessel nearly twice the *Hume*'s size, on Lake Erie in November 1879, illustrates a possible explanation of the *Hume*'s loss. Bound for Buffalo on the sixteenth of the month, the *Breed* was sailing with a brisk wind when she was overtaken by a powerful squall, tragically rolling her over. Only two of eight crewmembers survived. Interestingly, after posing on her beam end for twenty minutes, she sank. As she foundered, she righted herself and settled to the bottom on an even keel. Unlike the *Hume*'s predicament, the *Breed* went down in shallow water and her spars remained visible above the surface of Lake Erie. Again, there was the wreckage issue: bedding, furniture and assorted wreckage littered the scene of the *Breed*'s demise.

To a pod of grizzled old mariners in Chicago chewing the loss of the *Hume*, neither the collision nor the squall theory was satisfactory. The stupefying absence of wreckage so puzzled them that they offered their own explanation: the *Hume* sailed to some obscure port, was repainted and renamed, and was trading elsewhere.

On July 14, almost two months following the *Hume*'s unsolved disappearance, the *Simmons* was some distance off Milwaukee on a glorious sailing day. Floating on the water was an object that captured the attention of the *Simmons*'s captain. It was a hatch cover, one he identified as being from the *Hume*.

The loss of the *Hume* remains as much a mystery today as it did to the old graybeard mariners discussing her loss at Chicago all those years ago. It may be poetic that her exit—however it came—duplicated her quiet, unobtrusive life. It should be added to the record, however, that a schooner discovered on the lake bottom in the path the *Hume* would have traveled is quite likely her. No positive identification can irrefutably be made on the wreck, discovered around the 1990s, and even the date of discovery is uncertain.

The Life of the *Hattie A. Estelle*

It's unclear how many observers took note of the wire rigging sported by the schooner *Mary L. Higgie* as she sat atop the ways of the Hanson and Scove shipyard at Manitowoc, Wisconsin in the opening days of August 1872. We know at least one person did: the reporter for the *Chicago Inter-Ocean*, on hand to cover the launch. The *Higgie* was one of the early lake vessels to be so equipped; the concept and application of wire rigging were in their infancy. Another feature the reporter mentioned was something no one could see. The *Higgie* carried another technological advancement, a "patent double action force pump," in addition to her prosaic bilge pump.

The *Higgie* was constructed for the sum of $23,000 upon requisition of Chicago vessel owner James L. Higgie, and was named after his daughter. The ship was rated at 311 gross tons and 139 feet in length, with a beam of slightly over twenty-six feet, and drew eleven feet of water.

At five o'clock in the afternoon on August third of that year, the large crowd that had assembled erupted in cheers, shouts, and whistles as the new lake schooner was introduced to her fresh-water element with an impressive splash. Unbeknownst to the celebrating throng that afternoon as the *Higgie* took to the water, her future travels would merit an encore round of applause. For nineteen years of her destined life, the exploits and peregrinations of the schooner and the people to sail her would leave us a vividly colorful historical legacy to rank with that of any vessel built on the Great Lakes. Adventure, triumph, and tragedy would underpin the story of the sailing vessel that the crowd cheering her inauguration at Manitowoc could not foresee.

Immediately, the *Higgie* and her first commander, Captain Thomas Moore, would receive their first "baptism" by weather on the lakes. The *Higgie* was caught in a screaming gale on Lake Michigan that raged September 28 and 29, causing widespread damage and destruction. The *Higgie* lost her centerboard in the storm, forcing her to return to the builders in Manitowoc for replacement. Given the lateness of the season, by the time the schooner reentered service her first year of operation was short. She spent her first winter lay-up at Chicago, as she almost invariably would for the duration of her career.

Although the boat was largely intended for the grain trade, James Higgie would also ship lumber and rare iron ore cargoes on her. By the latter part of April 1873, the ship had loaded twenty-one thousand bushels of corn at Chicago, awaiting opening of the navigation season. Also awaiting the *Higgie*, and for that matter the economic climate of the entire nation and Western Europe, was the looming dark menace of the Panic of 1873.

Historian David Blanke called the Panic of 1873 "the first global depression brought on by industrial capitalism." He points out that the most developed nations in Europe and North America could invest their money in international currencies, backed by specie, making comparisons on currencies comparable even across the wide ocean.

On both sides of the Atlantic, in the port cities of various nations, the economy and currencies strained and faltered. Some collapsed and never recovered. Jay Cooke and Company's railroad-building empire was ostensibly to blame for the woes of the United States. Another timely culprit was Germany's decision to withdraw its venerable coinage from the silver market, shifting to the gold standard. The gold market exploded, the silver market sagged, and the silver became less valuable than the perspiration expended to mine and mint it.

Against this gloomy economic backdrop, rays of hope—golden shafts of light—would pierce the despair. In European cities there was a healthy demand for hardwood and softwood from North America—particularly from the Great Lakes states, and specifically from the states of Wisconsin and Michigan. A small group of savvy vessel owners and operators along with lumber barons recognized this windfall market and were quick to exploit it.

At Quebec, far up the St. Lawrence River, agents for trans-ocean shipments congregated. With the collapse of the silver market, often the incentive to paying off vessels just to reach Quebec was gold. The enticement was obvious to vessel owners in the challenging economic times that prevailed.

The lure of impending lumber profits in these times of domestic stagnation captured James Higgie's attention. Near the middle of October 1876, the *Higgie* was loading lumber at Manistee, Michigan, destined for that El Dorado of Canadian cities, Quebec. As she set sail, she was trailed by another schooner on the same mission, the *City of Green Bay.* They met with foul weather on Lake Erie, during which the *Higgie* lost her mizzenmast sails. Undaunted, and after the time-consuming transit of the Welland Canal, the duo set sail for Kingston, Ontario. After discharging their cargoes, given the lateness of the season, the intended trip to Quebec was truncated at Kingston. Both boats then retraced their course back to Chicago, where they would settle in for winter lay-up.

Early in June 1877, James Higgie and Chicago cohort and vessel fleet owner David Dall arrived in Quebec. The market for lumber and hardwood was still propitious, and both men sat at the roundtable of negotiations to send their vessels to sea. Dall decided to send his schooner *Summer Cloud* and James Higgie his daughter's namesake. Days after returning to Chicago, James Higgie announced to the press that the *Higgie* would depart for Europe on the twentieth of June. He also announced who the captain of this promising and bold undertaking would be: Captain H. J. Hatch, a young Chicagoan and father of five.

As the news of the *Higgie*'s imminent departure was published, the lake schooner *City of Manitowoc* was set to depart Quebec for Scotland, where her cargo of elm and pine lumber was calculated to bring a return on her freight of nearly $4,000 in gold. One can envision James Higgie and Dall rubbing their hands together, smirking.

When the *Higgie* set sail from Quebec, bound for Gloucester, England, she did so with lumber loaded at Oconto, Wisconsin. Upon reaching the cold, salty water of the North Atlantic, her wind-borne journeys began. She would cross, then recross the Atlantic, and repeat. With Quebec the nearest she would get to the Great Lakes for the next two years, she would touch base just long enough to load another lumber shipment from Michigan or Wisconsin, then raise her sails again to the ocean winds. Upon completion of a flawless if unremarkable voyage to Gloucester and divesting her lumber cargo, she skipped up the coast of the Bristol Channel to Swansea, Wales. She hunkered under the coal chute to load a consignment to be delivered back at Quebec. She arrived in mid October.

On October 23, 1877, the *Higgie* departed Quebec for a second time, laden with lumber from a Great Lakes state. As such, her Atlantic Ocean tramping would expand, building her reputation and travel portfolio, which would captivate the citizens and sailors of port cities throughout the lakes region when her story would be published in the *Chicago Inter-Ocean* two years later.

The schooner's destination was the fascinating unknown of Cape Town, South Africa. Again, she arrived safely and unloaded, then reloaded what may be the most improbable shipment ever carted aboard a Great Lakes vessel to that time—and some time beyond—when she took on supplies for the British army in South Africa. Upon delivery at East London, South Africa, her ability to hustle up peculiar cargoes was manifest. Shackled and marched aboard the *Higgie* were prisoners of war to be delivered to Cape Town. Back at East London, the *Higgie* loaded a more conventional cargo—certainly not by Great Lakes commodities standards—wool. Thereupon she set sail again for Quebec.

It would be 1879 when the *Higgie* arrived at Toulon, France, shouldering what would be her final load of lumber shipped from the Great Lakes states. When she cleared her hold, she sailed light from Toulon out the Mediterranean Sea through the Straits of Gibraltar to Cadiz, Spain. At Cadiz she loaded salt. When she raised anchor to sail once more, her destination this time—at last—was Chicago.

The *Higgie* arrived back at Quebec on September 3, 1879. Her salt cargo had to be lightered by seventy tons to permit her to transit the Welland Canal. She reached Detroit on the twenty-second, nestling into a dock along the hectic river. This was no quotidian docking of yet another of the seemingly countless sailing vessels to ply the lakes, and as Hatch stepped from the ship he was immediately besieged by friends and folk alike who appreciated maritime exploits and accomplishments. The safe return of the *Higgie* set off a boisterous welcome. There was an equipment matter needing attending to as well when the schooner tied up at Detroit. The *Higgie*'s mainsail had been blown away in the Gulf of St. Lawrence. She had also lost her centerboard, as she had done in her first blow, fresh from the builder's in 1872.

Departing Detroit, the *Higgie* moved up to Cheboygan, Michigan. Here her salt cargo was relieved. Much more familiar was the lumber load she took on; now her course was set for the Straits of Mackinac and on to Chicago. She dragged ponderously through the water: not because of the deck load of lumber she shipped, but by virtue of barnacle encrustation and the beard of seaweed that streamed from her keel.

On the eighth of October, the *Higgie* lashed to her dock on the Chicago River, to unbridled celebration. The years away from home had ceased. Family and loved ones, friends and neighbors, and any soul appreciating a good seafaring story mobbed the dock, welcoming the crew home. Calling it merely a hero's welcome would be understated, as it marked her arrival back to the port from which she so proudly hailed.

Extended voyages to foreign lands and strange port cities did not give the *Higgie* the right to rest on her laurels. Being championed for her remarkable accomplishments and resumé, worthy and proud, didn't comport with the schooner's role: a working ship. The ship was dispatched to a drydock to have her keel scraped. In almost no time at all she was back on the Chicago-to-Buffalo grain run, on which she would close out the 1879 shipping season.

When the *Higgie* emerged for the 1880 season, Captain Frank Higgie had taken charge of her. Frank Higgie was James Higgie's nephew. Why he was tabbed to replace Hatch isn't clear. Frank Higgie was no less accomplished, however, for he had command of the *City of Manitowoc* when it went to sea in trans-ocean lumber ventures, like what the *Higgie* had been engaged with. What we do know is that on June 6, 1880, the *Higgie* was downbound on Lake Michigan, wheat laden for Buffalo, when a furious late-spring gale dropped over the lake. She was stripped of her mainmast, foretopmast, and much of her canvas by the time she ducked into Manitowoc, the port of her genesis, for shelter. That day on storm-wracked Lake Michigan caused more damage to the *Higgie* than she had sustained in more than two years sailing the Atlantic Ocean.

Now that she was back on the lakes, the *Higgie* would continue to shadowbox with fate. Early May 1882 was cold and dank on portions of the upper lakes; blustery northern winds and depressing iron-gray skies had prevailed since late April. On Tuesday night, May 9, 1882, the *Higgie*, with a partial load of iron ore in her hold, ran aground on Pilot Island, at the entrance of Green Bay. When she rumbled to a halt, she was in four feet of water on a rocky bottom. She gouged herself open in the process, flooding her hold and the ore cargo.

The wrecking firm of Atkins and Beckwith was contracted by Higgie to release the schooner, and with an outfit of steam pumps, hawser, tackle, and so forth placed aboard the steam barge *Emma E. Thompson*, the salvagers departed Chicago. Ten days after finding the rocks at Pilot Island, the *Higgie* was released.

She was towed to Milwaukee and on May 22, drydocked there. The extent of her damage was considerable. She needed new planking on her starboard side forward, a portion of her keel replaced, and extensive caulking, resulting in a significant repair bill.

Two years later, the *Higgie* was upbound on Lake Michigan bound for Chicago under full canvas. She was unwieldy after a heavy squall filled her sails and she collided with the year-old tugboat *Duncan City.* The contact issued heavy damage to the tug's bow while relieving the *Higgie* of her jibboom, bowsprit, and headgear.

On October 1, 1886, the *Higgie* was docked at Buffalo near the Ohio Street bridge. Nearby was the veteran schooner *Newsboy*. Alma Huginson, a mate on the *Higgie*, and Abram Anderson, a sailor on the *Newsboy*, took to conversation. With few exceptions, the reports of the events to follow, as found in the newspapers, are vague, if not inscrutable. The friendly chat invited having a few drinks. Or quite a few. Then, through the wonders of alcohol, things may have gotten steamy and run afoul. They may have argued. What became certain would be Huginson falling into the Buffalo River and drowning and Anderson being arrested. He would be released a few days later when no evidence of foul play was discovered. By the actions of the transparent hand of fate, the *Newsboy* and *Higgie* would share calamity in the future, and once again it would be the people from the *Higgie* who suffered the greatest consequences.

Higgie sold the durable *Higgie* in 1888 to another Chicagoan. Captain Delbert Estelle paid the sum of $8,000 for the boat. He too chose a love in his life for whom to rename the schooner, his wife Hattie, and the ship sailed as the *Hattie A. Estelle.*

Late in the spring of 1889 the schooner would meet her most serious brush with disaster thus far in her seventeen years of service. On May 30, loaded with iron ore from Escanaba, Michigan, the *Estelle* was downbound on Lake Huron, battling a strong northeast wind as she sailed for Sandusky, Ohio. Troublesome seas were building, and that afternoon, off Thunder Bay Island, the *Estelle* fell into the trough of the seas, a dreaded occurrence all mariners fear. Her foremast went, breaking into three pieces and taking with it her main and mizzen topmasts. One of the heavy sections slammed to her deck, opening a large hole that permitted boarding waves to pour in as they rolled over her.

The *Estelle*, no match for the tempestuous Lake Huron, was driven aground near Thunder Bay Island. When the schooner was sighted, clearly in danger, her plight was relayed to the Thunder Bay Island Life-Saving Station by the assistant lightkeeper of the island's lighthouse. With great difficulty the lifesaving crew rowed out to the stricken *Estelle.* The condition of his schooner dictated to Delbert Estelle and the lifesavers to secure the services of a tug and get the *Estelle* into safe anchorage as soon as possible. Aware of the tug *Mocking Bird* at anchor in the bay, the lifesavers returned to secure her service. They succeeded, and with their lifeboat in tow of the *Mocking Bird*, set out once more for the imperiled schooner. Barely underway, they met with her under the tow of a large, unidentified steamer that towed the *Estelle* into sheltered waters. High winds ripped through the damaged *Estelle*'s broken rigging the next day, whipping pieces of her spars from the stays, making it too dangerous to board her. When the winds subsided later that night, she was towed to Alpena, Michigan, for repairs.

Life for Delbert Estelle and the storied schooner moderated for a while. At a grain elevator on the Chicago River in the lateness of day on November 15, 1891, one can imagine a pensive Delbert Estelle as his ship was loading. We cannot know what occupied his thoughts that day. The potential perils of navigating on the lakes in November certainly had to cross his mind. The weather that evening as the *Estelle* was loading was tolerable enough, even when she was ready to cast off. As the schooner left Chicago, heading up Lake Michigan, and the breeze freshened into a steady wind, Delbert Estelle likely never envisioned that the venerable ship he sailed was cashing in the last of her chips; her fortunes were about to play out.

Buffeting her about as she started up Lake Michigan on Monday, November 16, for her long-familiar port at Buffalo, the westerly wind that pushed the *Estelle* gradually swung around to the northwest. As it did, it increased in velocity. Accompanied by falling temperatures, snow developed. By nightfall the conditions on Lake Michigan were execrable; a howling gale and snow squalls were creating havoc for mariners. As the *Estelle* fought her way up the lake, five schooners that had left Muskegon, Michigan, were enduring the same frightful weather Delbert Estelle was contending with on his boat. The *Penobscot, George L. Wrenn, Mary Collins, Rouse Simmons*, and *Cape Horn* were being pummeled by thundering seas bound for Chicago.

Upbound from Manistee, the tiny steam barge *Ida E.* was being assaulted, while a few hours behind her the steamer *Fayette* was subjected to the same treatment. As the plundering seas stripped the deck loads of lumber from the *Cape Horn* and the *George L. Wrenn*, the punishing waves froze to decks and cabins of the *Fayette*, eventually freezing shut her pilothouse door. When the sun rose on Tuesday, the storm wailed on without sign of abatement. The *Estelle* was groping her way up the eastern shore of Lake Michigan when a leak was discovered. If the *Estelle* was still equipped with the "patent double action force pump" she proudly boasted of at her launching nineteen years prior, it failed her—it froze. That afternoon the *Estelle*, waterlogged and steering wildly, was forced to make a very risky attempt to enter the piers at Manistee. As Delbert Estelle was aiming for the schooner's last shot at refuge, the *Cape Horn*, leaking and less her deck load of lumber, had reached the safety of Chicago. Conversely, at the entrance to Green Bay on South Fisherman's Shoal, the schooner *Newsboy* ran aground and was in mortal danger.

The lifesavers at the Manistee station watched as the *Estelle* neared the piers, poised with heaving lines in the event that she successfully negotiated the channel. Ironically, the schooner's centerboard, which she lost at inconvenient times in her career, could not be extracted, most likely because it too had iced. When it became evident that the *Estelle* was not going to make it through the channel safely and would ground north of the piers, the lifesavers hastily returned to the station for the surfboat.

When the *Estelle* came in north of the piers, she swung about with her bow nosing shoreward. As her jibboom ranged over the north pier wall, turning back out to sea, one of her sailors, James Stone, made a death-defying leap from the boom to the pier and scampered to shore safely. Moments later the *Estelle* went aground hard with her bow pointed in to the southeast some thirty yards from the pier. The seas were massive, not only lashing over the ship's stern, but exploding off the pier and hammering back at the *Estelle*.

Volunteers from a large crowd assembled on the beach aided the lifesaving crew in attempt to launch the surfboat. Aboard the frangible *Estelle*, crewmen rushed forward as the aft cabin of the schooner was blasted by murderous waves. Seaman Albert Davis became entangled in the *Estelle*'s anchor gear, and as waves swept over him, he fell and broke his leg. Utterly helpless, Davis died a gruesome death in the forecastle of the *Estelle* as the lifesavers' surfboat was repeatedly ineffective and rebuffed from reaching the broken boat so frustrating and maddeningly close to shore.

Delbert Estelle remained aft to comfort the schooner's cook, Annie McGovern, as the lifesavers, unable to successfully launch the surfboat, erected the Lyle gun for shooting a line to the *Estelle*. The main, fore, and headsails of the *Estelle* were still set, and although an unimpeded view of her was lacking, the lifesavers and congregation of onlookers ashore could see the schooner's crew knotted in the forecastle. The trajectory of the Lyle gun was aimed low to reach the men huddled in the *Estelle*'s bow. Too low, and it fell short of the mark.

With the failure of the Lyle gun and the surfboat ineffective, a heaving line was at last successful in reaching the doomed *Estelle* and the breeches buoy was employed. One man from the schooner's crew was safely brought in, explaining as he landed the plight of Delbert Estelle, the cook, seaman Davis, and the two remaining crewmen forward on the boat. As the *Estelle* pounded in the roaring surf, Surfman Andrew Landell was sent out in the breeches buoy to aid the remaining crew stranded in the bow. About this time, the punishment the *Estelle* was subjected to overwhelmed her and she broke in two between her main and mizzen masts. The heroic efforts of Landell placed the two sailors in the forecastle of the *Estelle* into the breeches buoy and safely ashore. He was unable to assist Davis, by then already dead. Annie McGovern was nowhere to be seen. Exposed to the elements and freezing to death, Delbert Estelle clung to the mizzen rigging while the Lyle gun, which had filled with ice, was taken to the station to be thawed and lifesavers formulated the next rescue plan. It came too late. Two more launches of the surfboat failed, and Delbert Estelle lost his grip on life, falling from the rigging and perishing in Lake Michigan.

When Delbert Estelle's and Annie McGovern's bodies were recovered from the beach south of the piers the following day, the press in Manistee scalded Captain John Hansen and the lifesavers for their perceived ineptness. The accusations in the press so impugned the Manistee Life-Saving Station that an investigation was ordered. As controversy swirled around the rescue attempt of the *Estelle*, the tug *Monarch* removed the crew of the *Newsboy*, gathered in the chain locker where they had been for two days, subsisting on her wet corn cargo for food. Like the *Estelle*, the *Newsboy* was a total loss.

Lieutenant H. B. Rogers, in charge of the Lake Michigan lifesaving stations, arrived at Manistee to look into charges of negligence regarding the *Estelle* wreck that boiled invective in the Manistee newspapers. Upon returning to Chicago following his investigation, Rogers was cornered by a reporter from the *Chicago Inter-Ocean* and gave the following statement of his visit to Manistee: "It seems to me that Captain Hansen and his crew of lifesavers worked faithfully and at great peril to their lives, and deserve praise instead of censure."

No praise came from Manistee, however, and none from Chicago when Delbert Estelle was laid to rest in his hometown. Under circumstances eerily similar to what befell the *City of Green Bay* four years earlier, the globe-trotting *Estelle* ended her days in shallow Lake Michigan water where people died, and the lifesavers were looked upon with contempt.

While Delbert Estelle's mourners attended his funeral, the whaleback steamer *Charles W. Wetmore* sat off the coast of California. As she was bound at that point for San Francisco and earning the distinction of being the only whaleback to round Cape Horn, a connection between this peculiar indigenous Great Lakes vessel and the broken remains of the *Estelle* would seem unlikely. Not necessarily so, for among the *Wetmore*'s crew of twenty-two was a captain from Chicago, a father of five whose name was Hatch.

The *W. H. Gilcher* Goes Missing

Much darker in contrast to the sheet-metal gray skies of the boreal chill and impending winter at Cleveland, Ohio, the 318-foot steel hull seemed to stretch endlessly against the skyline. It was one week before Christmas in 1890 as the vast crowd that had assembled at the Cleveland Shipbuilding Company marveled at the Goliath freighter atop the stocks awaiting launch. The temperature was at the freezing mark, but on a day bristling with civic pride for the coming launch of the largest vessel to be built at Cleveland, the mood and jubilation of the occasion rendered the unappealing weather insignificant. At three o'clock sharp, the yet-unnamed freighter slid evenly from the ways into the Cuyahoga River, in a textbook launch.

The steamer, an engineer's delight built for the Gilchrist Transportation Company, featured steam capstans fore and aft with additional steam plants for hoisting on her spar deck. Externally, she was a duplicate of the steamer *Western Reserve*, launched from the same yard a few months prior, but could boast of an additional eighteen feet of length. Her power plant was slightly smaller: a triple expansion engine fed by twin Scotch boilers that ultimately turned a single propeller, twelve feet nine inches in diameter. To complement her length, the boat had forty-one feet beam and drew twenty-four feet of water. Payloads would come by virtue of coal cargoes she would move up the lakes and grain shipments down. Finish-up work could proceed in leisurely fashion, with the winter setting in.

Early in 1891 the formidable black hull carried a name, *W. H. Gilcher*, and a crew had been selected to her appointment. Leeds H. Weeks of Vermilion, Ohio, was named captain, a man of long standing in the Gilchrist Fleet, with Sidney B. Jones as chief engineer.

Expectations for the *Gilcher* were understandably lofty. Besides being the largest vessel ever built at Cleveland, the boat would be among the largest plying the lakes. Her emergence came at a time when shipbuilders were still producing wooden vessels, and the facile industry of steel construction hadn't entirely thrilled shipbuilders everywhere, nor the people who sailed them. The *Gilcher*'s consortium of owners investing in her was firm in the belief that the steel-hulled freighter was the future in Great Lakes shipping.

The *Gilcher* was quick to oblige her owners. On her second trip, the big steamer pulled away from Buffalo on Wednesday June 3, 1891, with 3,150 tons of coal in her capacious hold. Bound for Chicago, the coal cargo was the largest ever carried on the lakes. It proved to be a bellwether of the summer to come for the boat: huge payloads, brimming profits, and broad smiles from her owners. By autumn the pendulum would swing somewhat, and the *Gilcher*'s armor of efficiency was shown not to be impregnable.

On October 10, locked down from the Soo, Weeks checked down the *Gilcher*'s speed, allowing the vessel following her, the *Susan E. Peck*, to pass. As the *Peck* moved ahead of the *Gilcher* in the Lake George Flats of the St. Mary's River, the upbound tow of the *Aurora* and the schooner/barge *George W. Adams* was converging at the same spot. Too much slack in the *Adams*'s towline allowed it to drift into the *Peck*'s lane, ramming and sinking the *Peck* in a matter of minutes. Traffic both up and downbound on the river came to a halt as the sunken *Peck* blocked the shipping lanes. The *Gilcher* had allowed the *Peck* to pass her just before the river-jamming collision, owing to the first instance of recalcitrance from the behemoth *Gilcher*: trouble with her rudder. Weeks chose to wait for a fleet sister ship and his former charge, the *J. C. Gilchrist*, to accompany his steamer down; a troublesome rudder in the close confines of the St. Mary's River was courting disaster. With navigation in the river temporarily shut down, Weeks's and the *Gilcher*'s wait exceeded what was desirable.

As winter closed in and the *Gilcher* went into lay-up, her rudder flaw outweighed the successes in her inaugural season. By mid April 1892 the big steamer was being fitted out for her second season. What fate had in store for the *Gilcher* could not have been foreseen in the wildest of imagination, not even with her season-opening trips of malfunction and bad luck.

On April 20, the *Gilcher* was upbound, coal laden, on the St. Clair River, below Port Huron. Like the St. Mary's River, the St. Clair River bore heavy ship traffic, and collisions were frequent. When the *Gilcher*'s steering chain parted that day, there must have been a heart-stopping moment for Weeks as his monster freighter drifted unmanageably. She avoided colliding with another craft, but ran aground on the Canadian side of the river and stuck fast.

Permits were issued to American tugs to release the stranded boat, and for three hours a trio of tugs pulled on her to no avail. The following day the tugs *Castle* and *Howard* made another attempt to yank the steamer free but failed. On April 22, after three hundred tons of coal being lightered from her hold, she floated again. She suffered no structural damage, and with the steering chain repaired she was quickly back in service. With another fleet sister ship, the *R. E. Schuck*, she headed for Duluth, where the two were chartered by the Gilchrist Transportation Company to ship wheat to Buffalo.

The impenetrable ice floes clogging the entrance to Duluth harbor had been mitigated somewhat following heavy rain. A switch of wind direction to the southwest aided in clearing away some of the ice trouble spots. Yet another Gilchrist steamer, the *Neosho*, bulled a chute into the port; the *Gilcher* was third in line behind the vessels *St. Lawrence* and the *Brazil*, and followed by an inspiring parade of twenty-nine other wooden-hulled steamboats and steel whaleback barges. The departure from Duluth brought more misfortune and her costliest repair bill. Grain-laden and circumfused by ice, trying to muscle her way through, the *Gilcher* stripped all the buckets from her propeller. Helpless once again, she was taken in tow by the *R. E. Schuck* all the way to Buffalo, where her cargo was unloaded and her crew replaced.

On August 30, 1892, *Gilcher*'s sister ship *Western Reserve* broke in two and foundered during a late summer gale on Lake Superior. Only one person survived the disaster, wheelsman Harry Stewart. It sent shockwaves through the maritime community. Here was a new steel-hulled mammoth freighter, a pioneering vessel in the developments of this new shipbuilding technology, erased with sobering loss of life during an imposing but not legendary storm.[1] When the *Gilcher* pulled away

1. The steel used in the construction of both the *Gilcher* and *Western Reserve* has for generations been the subject of interest and speculation. I choose not to enter the debate. My intention is merely add to the *Gilcher*'s story prior to the loss and repercussions and reactions following.

from Chicago on September 14 with 118,885 bushels of corn in her hold, a record cargo carried by a lake boat, it earned but a tiny blurb in the marine news column of the *Chicago Inter-Ocean*, as the shock of the loss of the *Western Reserve* hung like funeral bunting over the Great Lakes shipping concerns.

It appears doubtful that Weeks held any suspicions regarding the seaworthiness of his charge. Late in October his only son, a second engineer by trade, was scheduled to rendezvous with the *Gilcher* at Buffalo and join her ranks. He arrived late and missed the boat, and if Weeks expressed disappointment in his dilatory son, Mrs. Weeks would be eternally grateful. It saved their boy's life.

On the blustery afternoon of Friday, October 28, 1892, the *Gilcher* was logged passing the Straits of Mackinac, bound for Milwaukee with another of her famed three thousand–plus coal cargoes. She never arrived at Milwaukee and hasn't been seen since. Committed to the upbound course to Milwaukee, the ship was sailing into the teeth of a storm of great force, a storm that would howl not only through Friday, but the next day as well. The tentacles of the blast were far reaching, disrupting shipping and distributing random destruction on Lakes Superior and Erie, as with Lake Michigan. For the second time—a very brief time—in lake's history, steel-hulled gargantuan freighters were humiliated by the abject forces of nature.

By Friday evening the intense gale began picking off schooners and steamboats and flicking them like lice onto beaches and against piers. Lifesavers at the North Manitou Island station on northern Lake Michigan hastened to the aid of the steamer *Maggie Thompson* and her consort, the schooner *Waukesha*, as they dragged their anchors and were in peril of being dashed ashore. Not far away, at Frankfort, Michigan, the schooner *Lincoln Dall* went on the beach, while further north, at Northport, the *Lizzie A. Law* was driven ashore. Off Manistee, the *Delos De Wolf*'s canvas was blown away and the lifesavers from the Manistee station performed a daring rescue of the small schooner *Michicott*, which had been stranded near the beach.

Later that night another small schooner, the *Nellie Hammond*, tried to make her way through the channel at Muskegon and into the safety of her harbor, to escape the gigantic seas. She struck the north channel wall, ripping a hole in her side. Two of her crew leaped to the pier and were saved, but the *Hammond*'s captain, Louis Nicholson, was lost. Throughout the night the storm raged on, and with morning's first light peering through the tattered clouds of dismay, the surface of the lake boiled. The severity of the tempest on Lake Erie was equally astonishing. Two large, steel-hulled ore boats, the 300-foot *Pontiac* and the 290-foot *Maruba*, were driven ashore near Cleveland, leaving mouths agape.

As October 1892 was peeled from the calendar, reports began stacking up on the desks of vessel operators and insurance underwriters. Various craft from sheltered areas began resuming voyages, while wrecked and damaged boats were undergoing salvage operations. Back at North Manitou Island, the steam barge *Pawnee* left the island's refuge to search for two schooner/barges it had released during the height of the storm.[2] Not far north of the island the *Pawnee* passed through a rather large quantity of wreckage that included furniture, bedding, stanchions, and other debris. When news of the *Pawnee*'s discovery reached the newspapers, speculation ran rampant.

As vessel salvage was underway, early November would see many boats, after being delayed by the fierce storm, begin reaching their destinations. At Chicago, another of the Gilchrist fleet, the *City of Rome*, reached her dock. The crew of the steamer reported that for many hours during the blow the forward and aft crewmen were unable to remain in contact with one another, owing to the kilotons of water that swept the deck. The steamer *John F. Eddy* and tow, the schooner *John Shaw*, which had also sheltered at the Manitous during the storm, reached Chicago the same day. The *Shaw*'s captain, George Dennis, stated that off the Manitous they too had passed through a vast field of wreckage, corroborating the discovery reported by the *Pawnee*.

Dennis's account listed even more wreckage, including doors, stools, window sashes, and part of a steamer's bridge with the bell still intact. "We could see nothing of which would give us any indication of what the name of the unfortunate craft was," Dennis told reporters. Dennis also reported the remains of an unknown schooner: a portion of her bilge and a bottom that had been freshly caulked. The sighting was off North Manitou Island, and quantities of hemlock lumber floated nearby.

With the *Gilcher* three days overdue at Milwaukee, the sobering prospect that the wreckage near the Manitous might be its remains rang through port cities along the lakes. Principal owners Frank W. Gilchrist and Joseph C. Gilchrist conceded on November second that hope had been lost for the *Gilcher* and her people. Joseph Gilchrist went to the home of Weeks in Vermilion to offer comfort and condolence to Weeks's wife.

On North Manitou Island, wreckage from the schooner *Ostrich* began coming

2. This was common practice on the lakes. It was held by most sailors that vessels were better off to fend for themselves in rough weather, rather than being lashed together with a tow line.

ashore. Given the close proximity of the schooner's wreckage and that of the *Gilcher*, a collision theory started to gain momentum. Some held the *Ostrich* and *Gilcher* came together at the height of the gale, dooming them both. A collision was certainly plausible. But could the *Ostrich*, roughly one-tenth the *Gilcher*'s tonnage, impact the big steamer enough to inflict a fatal blow?

The freshly caulked bottom that Dennis observed from the then-unidentified *Ostrich* told the tale of near disaster the ship had barely escaped the month before. On September 10 she came within an eyelash of foundering on the same lake. She was under the command of Captain John McCay, leaking drastically and flying distress signals, when spotted by the lifesavers of the Sturgeon Bay Ship Canal Station. When the lifesavers arrived, they relieved the schooner's weary crew and managed to keep her afloat. However, no amount of new caulking saved the *Ostrich* on the night of October 28.

At the offices of Moore, Bartow, and Gilchrist in Cleveland, where managing the travels of the Gilchrist boats was headquartered, telegrams were sent and arrived, all inquiring for any tidings of the *Gilcher* and her crew. A dispatch from Leland, Michigan, reached Cleveland on November third with the following message: "Furniture and wreckage has been picked up on North Manitou Island marked W. H. Gilcher. The steamer must have foundered on the night of October 28th, north of the Manitous." Partner John W. Moore mulled over the telegram and sadly added, "That dispels the one lingering hope we had left. I knew she was gone for if she wasn't, Captain Weeks would have taken her to port. The wreckage in the vicinity too, and the fact that no one sighted her bore positively against the supposition that she was safe, but it was hard to give up."

Although little publicized, Captain Duncan Corbett of the schooner *Waukesha*, which lifesavers at North Manitou Island had tended when the storm wailed, offered a revealing statement when the *Waukesha* finally reached its destination of Port Huron, Michigan. Corbett and the crew of the *Waukesha* announced that they had observed the lights of a large steamer, and witnessed those same lights disappear in the vicinity of South Fox Island, just north of North Manitou Island. Corbett's claim drew small audience, but the Cleveland Shipbuilding Company drew attention.[3]

With the wolf at the door, the defense of the Cleveland Shipbuilding Company

3. Lake Michigan would eventually claim the *Waukesha* as one of its victims. On November 7, 1896, the *Waukesha* sank off Muskegon, drowning six of her crew of seven, including Captain Duncan Corbett.

was assumed by President Henry D. Coffinberry. No puns were hurled at his name, which certainly lent itself to barbs, as two new three hundred–foot steel-hulled freighters lay silent as coffins on the bottoms of lakes Superior and Michigan. Adamant in the face of scorn, Coffinberry defended the *Gilcher*'s construction and that of the *Western Reserve.* "The Western Reserve and the Gilcher were the best steamers our company ever built," he claimed. When asked what caused the *Gilcher* to founder, he answered matter-of-factly, "She was either in a collision or on the rocks. No wind or sea could bother her loaded as she was."

Insurance on the *Gilcher* was handled by several carriers and divided into sums of $18,000 to $25,000 at firms in cities that included Chicago, Buffalo, and Milwaukee. One firm, which remained anonymous, reinsured its heavy risk on the *Gilcher* immediately following the loss of the *Western Reserve*, rejecting the notion that the *Western Reserve* was lost under an unusual combination of circumstances that had little likelihood of being repeated. The intimation was that the *Gilcher*'s construction paralleled that of the *Western Reserve*, and the question of steel used to build both vessels was suspect. The debate was hot for some time and historians today may advance the topic. So far as is known, there is no proof, but alas, the *Gilcher* is still missing. If the steel used in making the *Gilcher* was indeed brittle, could spearing by the *Ostrich* have done them both in?

The complete roster of the *Gilcher* is unknown. The exact number lost is also uncertain, but is generally believed to be between eighteen and twenty-one. Marine City, Michigan, was devastated by the disaster. Besides chief engineer Sidney B. Jones, second engineer Peter Shackett, oiler Charles Huntoon, and two brothers with the surname Hostler all hailed from the St. Clair River city. Others known to be aboard the ship were first mate Ed Porter, second mate Finley, a wheelsman by the name of King, an oiler identified only as Thompson, steward Charles Williams, and a fireman by the name of Green. Four unknown deckhands hired on at Buffalo to work the *Gilcher*'s last trip; thus, a bitter fate of first trip and last were wedded forever in some unknown spectral grave of Lake Michigan.

On November 9, the steam barge *Hattie B. Pereue* docked at Chicago, whereupon her master, Captain Stufflebeam, testified with further evidence of the sudden end of the *Gilcher.* Stufflebeam found the strongbacks that held the canvas covers of the steamer's lifeboats and they had been cut with an ax, indicating there was precious little time to escape before the steamer went into its death throes. By the end of the next week a message reached Cleveland that two bodies wearing life preservers from the *Gilcher* had washed ashore on one of the Fox Islands, not stipulating which island, north or south. Identified through papers found on them, they were the bodies of Williams and Green. Theirs were the only bodies ever recovered.

If the last human beings to see the *Gilcher* logged her past the Straits of Mackinac on October 28, 1892, or saw her lights disappear in the distance from the tumbling deck of the schooner *Waukesha* later that same night, that matters nothing. One thing is certain all these decades later: the *Gilcher* still hasn't been seen, as her final resting place on the bottom of Lake Michigan is unknown.

A Detestable Day Along the Chicago Lakefront

Maybe their names were elicited appealing imagery, like *Mercury, Rainbow, Myrtle*; pedestrian like *M. J. Cummings, Lem Ellsworth, Jack Thompson*; or tripped poetically from the tongue or teletype like *J. Loomis McLaren, Lincoln Dall, Moses Gage.* Perhaps this broad range of names adorning the sterns of sailing craft bound for destiny on Lake Michigan on the same day piqued my interest. Add their collective histories, some more colorful than their names. Overarching would be the cyclonic turbulent weather brewed over Lake Michigan, making their names secondary, at best, to their imminent destruction.

The day of May 17, 1894, temperatures over the Great Lakes region had soared into the mid eighties in many spots, sultry and perhaps indicative of the promise of what the coming summer would bring. The next morning all hell broke loose. A powerful low-pressure event bulled in from the Great Plains and collided with the high-pressure system that produced the unseasonably warm conditions. When they met, the ensuing chaos created by the dynamic forces was punctuated by a counterclockwise wind flow that would escalate to astounding, sustained wind speeds. Likewise, the temperature would plummet. In the span of seven hours at Port Huron, Michigan, the temperature dropped thirty-eight degrees. In the cities of Princeton and Woodstock, Illinois, the mercury dropped fifty degrees in twenty-four hours.

The flow of the system unleashing the strengthening winds from the north would sweep nearly the entire length of Lake Michigan. With the break of day at Chicago, the air temperature stood at thirty-seven degrees. Relentless winds from the north-northeast rarely dropped below forty miles per hour, and often gusted in blows above fifty: ideal conditions for generating massive and plundering seas that only the lakeshore at Chicago could absorb, as they roared down Lake Michigan.

In 1890, the Weather Bureau (a precursor to the National Weather Service) became a civilian enterprise, issuing flood warnings and fire forecasts. Valuable as early scientific weather advances were, the medium to communicate with ships at sea or isolated communities or rural townships was yet to come. Wireless and radio contacts were yet to be developed.

There would be a recurrent theme on this doleful day about to unfold on the Chicago lakefront. Many of these sailing ships about to be lost had found themselves in peril at other periods of their existence while working the lakes, and in many cases on Lake Michigan itself. They were no strangers to the potential dangers in horrible weather the lake could unleash. A fascinating angle to the demise of so many vessels in a single event is just how little about them and their histories has been recorded.

With shrieking banshee winds ripping away siding from buildings and lifting roofs, dropping tree limbs—if not uprooting entire trees—and raising ugly fifteen-foot seas, the southern waters of Lake Michigan provided the stage and denouement for several veteran players that had been paid little attention until this day. Soon thereafter, all but forgotten in the deep fjord of history. Morning at the lakefront would find some fifteen sailing ships precariously riding at anchor near the entrance to Chicago harbor, bows to the sea to meet the heavy rollers head-on. The lakefront feature Navy Pier was still years away at the time, and although a government pier had been constructed to break the waters of Lake Michigan in turbulent weather, gaining entrance to shelter in conditions such as these was treacherous. Ideally, if a boat could ride out the storm at anchor, that was the preferred method.

With Chicago the focus, what was happening just north at Milwaukee that wretched morning on Lake Michigan would signal what would be tallied at the end of the day. Around 9:30, the schooner *Cummings*, a twenty-year veteran, 137 feet, 330 tons, was wallowing and fighting her way toward the harbor entrance.

John McCulloch was her captain, and he and the crew of the *Cummings*, which was laden from coal taken on at Buffalo, knew that running through the piers was highly risky. Already flying the stars and stripes of the American flag inverted in show of distress, McCulloch avoided the piers, hoping to find the lee behind the south arm of the breakwall where the seas would be quelled. McCulloch had the ship's anchors dropped and briefly, for scarcely enough time to exhale, they held.

As her anchors slipped and pushed the *Cummings* toward the beach, the crew of the tugboat *Simpson*, alarmed by the danger to the schooner, chugged out of Milwaukee harbor in the hope of getting a towline to the *Cummings*. The *Simpson* had barely cleared the protection of the piers when she was ravaged. An uninterrupted wave boarded her stern, sending cascading green water into her engine room, threatening to snuff her boiler fire. She rolled and pitched like a poltergeist and her captain was forced to wrestle their way back into the harbor. When the *Cummings* stranded, with her stern finding bottom first, this came with such violence that the shock waves shattered her rudder casing, opening a massive hole through which water poured with alarming, unimpeded volume. In short order, the towering seas boarded her, forcing the crew into the mizzen rigging.

In the study of shipwrecked vessels stranded near the beach during the Gilded Age—the era of Lyle guns, breeches buoys and surfboats—one will find that the valor of lifesaving crews was thwarted by bad luck and maddening circumstance, inimical as the weather itself. Such misfortune and frustration would confront the rescuers and crew of the *Cummings*.

No sooner had the *Cummings* stranded when the surfmen of the Milwaukee Life-Saving Station, under the command of Captain Pratton, arrived with beach apparatus and assembled the noble Lyle gun. They fired one shot, and it fell so far short of the wreck that Pratton abandoned this idea. They hustled to the station for the lifeboat and Pratton solicited tugboat operators to tow them beyond the piers, including for the tugs *Knight Templar* and the foiled *Simpson*. Both declined. No doubt the people of the *Knight Templar* observed the earlier attempt by the *Simpson* and wanted no part of the foul lake that day.

After an unidentified tug finally did take the lifeboat's line, only to drop it, Pratton and his crew of seven lifesavers were forced to haul out to the *Cummings*, and miraculously converged with her. They were pulling alongside when a pugilist wave struck, driving the lifeboat into the schooner's rail. The lifeboat recoiled, and just before it overturned, a surfman by the name of Gerdes leaped aboard the *Cummings*. Like the crew of the schooner, he was forced to scramble to the mizzen rigging. Not only overturned, the station's lifeboat was damaged, but the men in the water would learn this only when they regained control of it. One intrepid lifesaver swam ashore. Being a powerful, durable swimmer was requisite to be a lifesaver, with the prowess of a Navy SEAL of the time. Those in the water eventually regained the lifeboat and managed to make shore. By the time they returned to the harbor, three hours had elapsed since the ineffective Lyle gun shot, and all that had been accomplished was losing the viability of the station's lifeboat and adding another person to the *Cummings*'s rigging.

Pratton hastily dispatched a telephone message, which had to be relayed to the Racine station, requesting the use of its lifeboat. Three hours later, when the boat arrived, it was the smaller, less effective surfboat, one of which Pratton already had at his disposal. He wailed in agony and disgust as the freezing crew of the *Cummings* began dropping from the rigging and drowning in the hellish seas.

It would take a lifeboat from the steamer *Nebraska*, in port at Milwaukee and offered for use to Pratton by her good crew, that would at last convey the lifesavers to the helpless *Cummings*. When they arrived, only the surfman Gerdes and sailor Robert Patterson were alive. Three others had fallen to their deaths; stewardess Elizabeth Palmer and sailor James Whitely had also died, remaining lashed to the *Cummings*'s rigging. Despondent, forlorn, exhausted, drenched, and inconsolable, Pratton and the lifesavers returned to the station in the *Nebraska*'s lifeboat. The disappointment about the ineffective rescue mission would soon boil over in a cauldron of criticism.

As one would imagine in the face of such a blow, forming a theater of so many bobbing and heaving sailing ships to behold, thousands of Chicagoans gathered at the lakeshore. Multiple dramas would unfold, and many of the assembled onlookers would leave behind their roles of mere spectators in order to assist potential rescue. Hoping and praying that anchors would hold their boats, the crew people aboard these craft, vessels with a combined sailing service of more than two hundred years, could do nothing, like those ashore, as events deployed. The *F. W. Gifford* and *Evening Star* were holding their own with others as the anchors of the *Rainbow* started to drag and lose contact with the lake bottom. Inbound were the *Myrtle* and *Thompson*, and with tens of thousands of board feet of lumber already plucked from the cast of schooners and agitating in the surf like action of an old Maytag washing machine, in these violently roiling waters the stage was set for the cataclysmic events about to take place.

Waterlogged in peril, what little canvas she had left in tatters, the *Myrtle* appeared to be running for the government pier. It soon became evident that the vessel was out of control, no matter the effort of her captain, Jerome Wilson, to corral her. Just outside the breakwall the *Myrtle* struck the *Evening Star*, carrying away the latter's jibboom and foretopmast. Minutes later she fouled with the *Gifford* and ripped away her own masts. Briefly entwined, the *Myrtle* was soon swept toward the shore with only the stub of her after mast standing. William Smith, captain of the beefy tug *Perfection*, made an attempt to harness the whirling *Myrtle*, but the heavy seas and thrashing lumber and wreckage rebuffed this try. Smith docked his tugboat at the harbor entrance, near the annex station of the Life-Saving Service.

Smith seemed to intuit that he would be summoned for another round with the big lake. The year before, 1893, Chicago had been host to the World's Fair, the lavish and opulently spectacular Columbian Exposition. Jackson Park was the scene of the fair, and with the expectation of heavy steamer traffic converging on the event, a lifesaving station had been erected there. The original station at the mouth of the Chicago River near the lighthouse became known as the annex station. The greatest dramatics this day would occur closest to this annex station and the government pier.

Surfman Frank Fountain was in charge of the annex station; he and his lifesavers were returning for the third time that day with citizens rescued from small craft imperiled by the storm when the *Perfection* docked. Worn out from the day's miserable activities, Fountain and his men secured the line of their durable lifeboat to the tug and set out after the *Myrtle*. Barely having cleared the piers, the lifeboat was struck abeam by a towering wave, capsizing it. Ever so adroitly, Smith wheeled the *Perfection* about and the lifeboat righted, with some of the lifesavers clinging fast. Fountain and two others remained in the water for forty minutes before they could be pulled aboard the tug. Drained of energy and weak from immersion in the hypothermic cold waters of Lake Michigan, the lifesavers could not return to work and the rescue effort failed.

The *Myrtle* stranded off Harrison Street and disintegrated. The multitudes that had gathered were helpless to aid the ship, and the entire crew was drowned in the debris-choked surf before the horrified crowd. Old lake schooners that had survived so many prior pitched battles with Lake Michigan were finally going to lose the war.

The aged *Thompson*, out of control as the *Myrtle* had been, came rumbling in next. Hopeful of gaining a towline that never came, the *Thompson* sledgehammered the *Rainbow*'s bow with her own, dooming them both. Gulping aboard angry, foaming water and careening for the beach with her foremast broken, the *Thompson* struck bottom off Twenty-Sixth Street, very close to shore. When she grounded, her foremast broke free, tearing with it rigging as it toppled into the raging seas.

The *Thompson*'s crew huddled in the forecastle, showered by the waves, waves that had divested the ship of her lumber cargo. The *Thompson* was surrounded by boards and flotsam and detritus littered about by the forces of nature that fiendish day. From the city's Fourth Precinct, police and firemen, aided by scores of volunteers, set to a rescue plan.

When, after repeated futile attempts, a line pitched from the beach finally reached the *Thompson*, a sailor nimbly scrambled over the remaining lumber cargo and grabbed it. Next, a stronger hawser was sent out. As it was fixed to the *Thompson*'s stern steering post, the encouraged throng on shore erupted in cheers.

Slowly and with great peril, the crew of the schooner wrestled their way ashore via the hawser lifeline. As the *Thompson* pitched with the seas the people manning the line on the beach would yank the line taut, attempting to keep those being rescued out of the water. It was an extraordinary exhibit of heroic rescue by the citizens of Chicago. It would have been flawless and was soured only when one man of the *Thompson*'s crew, Charles Caucier, chose his own method to rendezvous with land. According to witnesses, Caucier sought to save himself by a log-rolling maneuver, hopping about the tangle of lumber clutching the ship. As the heaving lumber gave way, he succumbed in the heavy surf. The *Thompson* was rapidly breaking apart as attention was turned to the *Rainbow*.

Torn from her anchorage after the *Thompson* thundered into her, the 256-ton *Rainbow*, once lumber-laden from Menominee, Wisconsin, but now plucked clean to her varnished deck timbers, wallowed, then capsized some distance offshore in the vicinity of Twelfth Street. As she turned turtle, her people took to the rigging and shrouds and gunwale of the overturned craft, struggling and holding on for life and the promise of a better day.

The gallantry and resolve of Chicagoans to save the lives of so many in jeopardy of annihilation on Lake Michigan during this nightmarish day cannot be overstated. With steam up in his tugboat *Mollie Spencer*, Captain Charles Roach coaxed the tug out between the piers and into the walls of water threatening to snuff out the *Rainbow*'s hapless people. In a resourceful display of seamanship, Roach skillfully maneuvered the *Spencer* near the *Rainbow* and succeeded in getting a line to the *Rainbow*'s people in the water. In the harrowing moments following this umbilical connection, four from the *Rainbow* were hauled aboard the *Spencer*. As Roach came about to heave another line to the three remaining crewmen, a wave exploded like a depth charge over the *Spencer*, shattering her pilothouse windows. That was enough heroics for Roach. A job well done, he steered the bucking tug safely home to harbor.

Still clinging to the sinking *Rainbow*, which by then was drifting to her demise off Sixteenth Street, Captain John Pugh and sailors Tom Williams and Jack Knutson knew the schooner's final bell was ringing. In a frenzy, with time running out, they frantically worked on a makeshift raft. With remnants of wreckage jury rigged, they lashed themselves to it and cast off. From the shore, the crowd that had assembled cheered and motioned them on, as if they were thoroughbreds coming down the homestretch at Pimlico. When near the beach a citizen named William Havill, along with others, pulled Pugh, Williams, and Knutson to safety, euphoria reigned over the electrified crowd.

Captain Angus McDonald, a phlegmatic salt in command of the Western Transit Company's *Hudson*, was on Lake Michigan that day. The *Hudson*, a 304-foot, iron-hulled package freighter with passenger accommodations, had endured a beating, but we can be thankful for McDonald's droll wit. As the *Hudson* neared Chicago, steering erratically, there was no smoke issuing from either of her twin fore-and-aft smokestacks.

Drawing nearer still, it was evident that the *Hudson* was without her pilothouse. It had earlier been snatched away by the mammoth seas. She was in emergency backup mode, being steered at the stern, which accounted for her wild behavior, not to mention the lather she was taking from the seas. Below decks, a generous portion of the steamer's cargo had broken open during the violent trip. Barrels of flour, thrown about, spread their contents in the cargo hold. We can imagine the chaotic mess in the *Hudson*'s white-out hold.

Later that night, with his bruised and damaged steamer snug at a dock, McDonald would display sangfroid when questioned by a reporter about the loss of the wheelhouse: "Some people might call it a tidal wave, but I think it was just an ordinary wave which happened to be a little bit bigger than the others."[1]

Amid this cyclonic turmoil, when it would seem a given that any vessel afloat on Lake Michigan would be mauled, and just about the time that the schooners *Mercury* and *McLaren* were about to wreck, the doughty little *F. & P.M. No. 1*, with

1. Angus McDonald may have in subsequent years redefined or clarified his categorizing of waves. We don't know. What we do know is that on September 16, 1901, still in command of the *Hudson*, he went down along with the boat in a howling gale on Lake Superior that claimed twenty-four lives, including his own.)

her butterknife bow, snorted into view. She lined up and shot the piers with ease and suffered no damage at all on her trip up the lake from Ludington, Michigan.

The 230-ton *Mercury*, commanded by Captain Matthew Schuman, was the first of the schooners with a long adversarial history of navigating the Lake Michigan in times of treachery to finally succumb to the oft-heartless body of water. The *Mercury* had been perilously close to this outcome in the past, indeed. In November 1879 the *Mercury* battled the lake for two ungodly days during a furious gale, complete with towering seas and frigid temperatures. She went aground just south of Pentwater, Michigan. Raked by billowing seas, harsh wind, and freezing environs, ice built on her hull as the crew crowded around a galley stove for survival, nearer to perdition than to the comforting aroma of Johnny cake. Six years and one month later, she belatedly slouched into Chicago, iced over and free of her lumber cargo, which had been whisked away in a deadly storm that claimed the schooner *Orphan Boy* and her entire crew.

When the *Mercury*'s anchor slipped she was several hundred yards off Twenty-Fifth Street. Schumer and his crew had knotted in the ship's bow. Waving to the assembled mob scene of Chicago cheerleaders on the beach, who waved in return to the ship, the next stanza of heroics began. The enormous amount of board feet of lumber collecting along the shore, tangled, jackstraw, desultory, would be exclaimed about in both newspaper accounts and the official report of the Life-Saving Service. In the case of some members of the *Mercury*'s crew, it would be fundamental to their survival.

When a line at last reached the schooner, a line relentlessly worked by the lifesavers, a sailor on the *Mercury*, Tom Thurston, grabbed it, and leaping over the rail he darted, hopped, and clambered over the mad spikes of lumber and wreckage and made it home. His amazing rendezvous with terra firma was replicated by two more crewmembers. And when another line was made fast and the remaining crewmembers, including Captain Schuman, were saved, employing the same method that had rescued the survivors of the *Thompson*, the celebratory crowd's boisterousness echoed like a thunderclap.

The last of the *Mercury*'s people had only momentarily been landed when she began to break apart under the weight of the relentlessly pounding, heavy seas. As she was reduced to kindling, the *McLaren* was coming ashore just north of her. With a crowd of thousands of observers, awash in hubris and success, carrying them along, Nelson St. Peter of the Jackson Park Life-Saving Station and his crew situated near Twenty-Fourth Street and erected the Lyle gun. It required two shots, but the technological tool of the age struck paydirt, delivering a line that was soon made fast to the *McLaren*.

The *McLaren* grounded stern-first. One by one, the men of the doomed schooner, clustered at the stern, made their rendezvous with land. Some plunged into the surf near shore but were quickly pulled to safety by the raucous crowd. One crewman had died earlier in the day when struck in the head by a section of tow post that had broken free. This left seventy-two-year-old sailor Charles Brown. Reluctant to leave, a bag of clothing under his arm, Brown seemed paralyzed. As Brown agonized whether losing his clothes was worth the risk, with the gathered on the shore imploring deliriously for him to leave the ship, his standoff was resolved by better sense. He pitched his bundle and slid home to the rescuers. In retrospect, Brown could have saved his finest threads and his life, too, for later that afternoon the *McLaren* was high and dry on the beach, a complete wreck.

While Brown lost his duds and the schooner was scavenged, to the east, at Michigan City, Indiana, the *Gage*, which had been laden with shingles for the A. R. Colburn Company of Chicago, was working frantically to reach the shelter of Michigan City's harbor. Most of the Gage's deck load of shingles had long since been washed overboard, stolen by the mountainous seas, and her sails had been reduced to rags. Captain Hart, the *Gage*'s master, failed to get his vessel into safe harbor that day, like so many others, and the ship was tossed ashore west of the piers. Three hours and two trips in the station's surfboat later, the Michigan City lifesavers had performed a textbook rescue of the schooner's entire crew. A few hours later the *Gage* broke apart, and like the A. R. Colburn shingles, her parts mixed with the foaming surf.

Near One Hundredth Street at South Chicago, the *C. G. Mixer* was doomed. When it ran aground about five hundred feet from shore, the lifesaving group from the South Chicago station would implement and successfully use another of that era's tools of maritime support and rescue, the breeches buoy. Once the Lyle gun fired a true line to the *Mixer*, the device was set up and operated. The *Mixer*'s crew compliment was brought ashore in this method, the only occasion for this during the entire tenebrous day. The odd, cartoonish device was also effective. Like other craft about her, the *Mixer* was pounded to pieces by powerful waves off South Chicago.

How much more maritime brutality this grim day could administer was being shown. Two more ships had sailed for destruction, and if one can delineate reason or patterns of past encounters on this grand lake—a vast aquatic body of marvel and frequent mayhem—those past brushes with catastrophe should lead to their final outcomes this occasion, in this familiar natural condition.

For the *Dall*, hardship on Lake Michigan was a way of life. The *Dall* had certainly seen stable and profitable days for early owner David Dall, but vexation by Lake Michigan formed her crucible. She was blown ashore south of Muskegon during a whistling gale in 1881. Heavy weather rudely introduced her to the pier at Manistee in 1883. In 1884 the *Dall* was treated to a similar experience again at Muskegon in another bout of foul weather. In October 1892 the *Dall* was savagely beached on the lake in the same storm that sank the *W. H. Gilcher*, a fine, new, steel-hulled steamer whose loss shocked the Great Lakes community.

Samuel Johnson was her captain the day the knock-out punch came, just north of Evanston, Illinois, near Glencoe. By the time the *Dall* stranded on the sandy bottom off Glencoe, one of her sailors, Anton Gunderson, had already been lost overboard in the deadly seas. The *Dall*'s yawl had been torn away, her steering gear was disabled, and what canvas she retained was colorless strands. Her remaining crew had taken to the rigging refuge of her bare poles.

If something akin to intuitiveness could lurk in the oaken hull of a doomed schooner once again battling her nemesis, such that perhaps a homing device, unknown or unseen by mortals, could place the schooner in a location giving the greatest chance for deliverance of her people, so be it for the *Dall*. The location where the *Dall* would wreck was under the jurisdiction of Evanston Life-Saving Station and, moreover, Lawrence O. Lawson. Lawson had already earned the highest honor issued by the Life-Saving Service, the gold lifesaving medal, following the heroic and daring rescue of the steamer *Calumet* when it wrecked on Thanksgiving Day of 1889.

Lawson was aided by, and supported in cheers from, a vocal and diligent throng of Northwestern University students who helped launch the lifeboat into the turbulent lake. Lawson and his Evanston lifesavers worked their magic again, as if scripted. As the *Dall* succumbed, the lifesavers rowed home with the stricken crew. From the bluffs overlooking the rescue scene, the cheers of the Northwestern students momentarily muted the roaring surf.

In the aftermath of the storm the following day, large crowds again assembled along the lakefront. Through the tangles of wreckage, under the wooden breakwater and government pier, Lake Michigan still roiled, sending up frothy white water that splashed at the derelict ships and flotsam and lumber ubiquitous along the Chicago shoreline. Three bodies from the crew of the *Myrtle* were recovered that day, including that of Captain Jerome Wilson.

At Milwaukee, the bodies of Elizabeth Palmer and James Whitely were still lashed to the rigging of the broken *Cummings*, igniting a firestorm of protest that was directed at Pratton. The strong railing persuaded Lieutenant W. S. Baldwin, in charge of the Eleventh District of Life-Saving Service Stations, to which Lake Michigan stations belonged, to investigate. Baldwin would exonerate Pratton of any shortcomings or blame in the tragic *Cummings* affair. Early Sunday morning, May 20, the bodies of Palmer and Whitely were removed, but the bitterness leveled at the Milwaukee Life-Saving Station persisted.

Untold thousands of board feet of lumber were carted off to nearby residences. Ghoulish entrepreneurs were soon in business selling souvenirs from the wrecked schooners. Pulleys, canvas, tackle, stools, flags, and the compass box from the *Myrtle* were sold for handsome sums. Craftspeople fashioned the timbers from the ill-fated schooners into canes.

At Detroit, an anxious Henry Wineman Jr., was anxiously awaiting some word on his tardy boat, *Ellsworth*. He was probably confronting his greatest fear. He may have been aware of the *Ellsworth*'s earlier escapes from destruction on Lake Michigan: for instance, how the *Ellsworth* was scuttled near Green Bay, Wisconsin, after being brutally mauled on the big lake in the storm that sank the Goodrich steamer *Alpena* in 1880, with heavy loss of life.

From the time Wineman purchased the *Ellsworth*, a 138-foot, 342-ton product of the famed Wolf and Davidson shipyard of Milwaukee, he had engaged her in the stone trade from Upper Peninsula Michigan ports to Chicago, often to the Malone Stone Company. When the steamship *Caledonia* docked at Chicago on May 23, her charge, Captain Lyons, said this about the *Ellsworth*, having passed the schooner downbound from the Soo on the St. Mary's River: "I noticed that the Ellsworth was deeply loaded. In fact, she was nearly decks to the water, and I said to myself when we went by that if that boat gets in a good breeze, she will be in trouble. I thought she was dangerously overloaded."

The *Ellsworth* met with a "good breeze" all right. As she was heavily laden with stones in a fifteen-foot sea, Wineman's fears were fulfilled. Shortly after the *Caledonia* touched her dock in Chicago, a fisherman toiling off Waukegan, Illinois, recovered a red and black yawl with the name "*Lem Ellsworth*" painted on it. The stone-heavy schooner took a crew of eight to the bottom with her.

Eleven vessels became total losses that day, claiming the lives of twenty-two men and women. Rarely has so much tragedy been witnessed by so many, and rarely has so much triumph teamed with disaster. More rarely yet is it remembered.

The Saga of the *Red, White & Blue*

At some juncture in my Great Lakes history research, a person whose name I cannot recall, at a time I cannot recollect, alerted me to a reel of microfilm available for public consumption at the National Archives in Washington, DC: Reel T 729, Marine Casualties on the Great Lakes, 1863–1873. This recondite treasure was joyously explored: an unexpected catalogue and glossary for a researcher. Chronologically arranged, the vessel listings were written with elaborate flair in the Edwardian script of the era. From innocuous and benign encounters and mishaps to the foundering and disappearances with the losses of entire crews, the steady hand of the registrar was methodical and exact.

Many vessel names I had never heard or read before came to light. As the film rolled, with this archaic scroll of lake boats resurrected, some of those unfamiliar names would repeat in a later year or years, marking some other misadventure or hard luck. As a result of this celluloid tickertape of Great Lakes vessels gone awry, the anonymous became known in its absurdity. One such repeat offender was the bark *Red, White & Blue* (*RW&B*), with her noteworthy scrapes on the Great Lakes.

When you find mention of bark-rigged ships that plied the lakes, the chances are they were built before the mid 1860s. Fore-and-aft rigged schooners became common in lake trade because they were practical. The advantage square-rigged ships had when working the high seas wasn't necessary on the shorter sailing routes on the Great Lakes.

The *RW&B* was laid down at Madison Dock, Ohio, a littoral, forgotten spot where Cunningham Creek joins Lake Erie, midway between Ashtabula and Fairport. The vessel was built in 1863 by the brothers Bailey, Alanson, Daniel, and Emery. The Bailey brothers would build eight boats during their shipbuilding years at Madison Dock. In 1856, they launched their first, the *Wide Awake*, and in 1864 their last, the *Wake Up*. One can't help but think that the bookend names of their fruits of labor should be reversed.

Keeping tabs on the *RW&B* required diligence. Her peregrinations throughout the lakes were punctuated in oft-harrowing trials and mix-ups; some freaks of nature were thrown in, adding to her rich life. She would sail for thirty-two years, quite remarkable, particularly when one considers that this is the same length of time the *John B. Aird*, a recently scrapped modern Canadian lake boat, a 730-foot steel-motor vessel, would last.

She changed hands on multiple occasions throughout her career, including shortly after commission. Records and a sift of newspaper columns indicated that at least one of those owners—or partial owners—was in his own right a captain, and he had resigned himself to losing his life with the *RW&B* on Lake Erie during one of the assaults in heavy weather it endured. He wouldn't. The boat's time wasn't just then.

Documents show that the *RW&B* was built for James Butler of Buffalo, New York. Two years later, according to enrollment documents and information disbursed by the Milwaukee Custom House Registry, the bark was sold to Racine, Wisconsin, vessel owner James R. Slauson. The very next season, 1866, shows her back in Butler's possession for one last time and one last season. She was sold back to Wisconsin interests, Fitzgerald and Company, in 1867 and would stay in their fold, as nearly as I can determine, until 1882.

In a black-and-white reproduction of what is either a watercolor painting or a sketch of the *RW&B* in her bark-rigged period, she appears to have sported a tricolor, horizontally striped paint scheme. One would conclude, given her name and the color variance of the photo, that those colors would have been red, white, and blue.

The Racine *Weekly Advocate* reported in the August 30, 1865, edition that Slauson and Captain John W. Brown had indeed purchased the boat for $30,000 from Butler. The following year the same periodical reported on June 13 that Slauson's boat made its first appearance in Racine, with Captain Brown at the helm. The paper went on to say, "We understand she is the finest and largest vessel ever in this port. She will make a handsome addition to our grain fleet." If indeed the RW&B was at the time the largest vessel to call at Racine, it's fair to say she was hardly awe-inspiring in size. Relative to her time of construction, however, she carried impressive numbers. One hundred fifty-seven feet in overall length, with a thirty-foot beam and drawing thirteen feet of water, she netted 447 tons. Her payload capacity was eight hundred tons.

In the early morning hours of May 17, 1867, the RW&B and the schooner *Barbarian* were under tow of the tug *Sweepstakes* in western Lake Erie, close to the confluence of the Detroit River. The *Sweepstakes* had just entered service. Over the years the tug would prove not only durable, but a delight to the eyes. Her graceful lines were accented with a carved wing-spread eagle atop her ornate pilot house and filigree scrollwork rambling across her prow and bow stem. A month on the job, her captain's desire was to add a third boat to the string, the *Racer.* In the maneuver—which backfired—the *Racer* and RW&B "came together with great violence," according to the *Cleveland Plain Dealer. Racer* bore the brunt of the damage: twenty-four of her stanchions, bulwarks, rails, and plank-sheer on her port side were "carried away" and her foresail was damaged beyond repair. The bark lost her jibboom and bowsprit and damaged her head gear. The dawning of that day in the spring of 1867, the collision on Lake Erie, would set the tone for the career path the ship was embarking upon.

In April 1868, favorable winds blew to propel sailing ships on the lakes with the wings of Mercury, as they did when a lumber-laden RW&B made the transit from Buffalo to Port Huron, Michigan. She sailed from the former on Sunday and arrived at the latter on Tuesday. This is pointed out because later in her career the boat would find an occasion when wind, the force of nature required to move her, would prove fickle and unaccommodating.

Her fortunes wouldn't change following this impressive quick trip. After being divested of her lumber cargo at Port Huron, she was being towed out to Lake Huron when she struck a submerged obstruction. A short distance up the lake she began leaking quite alarmingly. By the time she put about and retraced her route to Port Huron, she had six feet of water in her hold. She was ministered to by steam pump and taken in tow by the *Leviathan* to Detroit for repairs. *Leviathan* and RW&B would renew their acquaintance later. By April 21, the damage to the bark was repaired—it was light—and she sailed from Detroit that evening.

A marine news brief in the *Cleveland Plain Dealer* from September 10, 1870, reported the *RW&B* in drydock at the Wolf and Davidson Shipyard in Milwaukee. No specifics were recorded. Late the following year, having left Milwaukee with a cargo of grain for Buffalo, she ran aground on High Island in northern Lake Michigan. On October 26, six days later, she was at Beaver Island for inspection, having been freed and towed by her familiar companion, the *Leviathan.*

Her growing affinity for islands studding the waterways of the Great Lakes and connecting channels would be noted a month later. On November 24, 1871, with a load of coal, she went ashore on Bois Blanc Island in the Detroit River. A couple of days later the tug *Wilcox* pulled her off. From a photo of the *Wilcox*, it was similar in appearance to the *Sweepstakes*: pretty boats for such rigorous work.

As gleaned from newspaper accounts, in the spring of 1872 the harsh winter weather held sway, reluctant to yield. A telegram from Buffalo received at Detroit on May 8 reported ice conditions off Buffalo. In part, it read: "A gentleman who reached this city to-day (Detroit), however, informs me that up to a late hour last evening no vessels had succeed in getting away from that port and that the departure of the steamers was much retarded by the solidity of ice, which has become but partially broken up." The telegram was forwarded to the desk of the marine correspondent of the *Chicago Inter-Ocean*, to which he added, "Thus far the Chicago downbound fleet have met with reasonable success in getting transferred through the Straits and St. Clair Flats, but such things are not without an occasional exception."[1] The telegram went on to say, "It is frequently asserted that there is not requisite caution carried out on the part of captains while crossing that thoroughfare—the water, as is well known, is quite shoal and in places vessels invariably steer wild (as the sailors term it) and the utmost caution has necessarily to be carried out."

There was plenty of activity on Saturday, May 4, 1872. Downbound and under tow, the *RW&B* and the *Maria Martin* were crossed up between tows and inelegantly rumbled into one another. This would be a common occurrence, even if the *RW&B* hadn't been involved. What was remarkable about the contretemps was that the *Maria Martin* was also a bark, and in my research over the years, this is the first instance I have discovered of two barks colliding on the lakes. Both barks sustained

1. The St. Clair Flats was the shipping channel from Lake St. Clair through the delta of the St. Clair River, newly created and a replacement for the original south channel. Predictably, the *RW&B* would provide one of the exceptions.

considerable damage. "Severe" damage to the *RW&B*, to her bow according to the Detroit *Tribune*, "obliged" her to call at the Campbell, Owen & Company dock at Detroit for repairs.

Five months later, on a Sunday morning in early autumn, the ship was bound for Buffalo. Briefly shimmering in the golden morning sun in a vision worthy of a Currier and Ives lithograph, the *RW&B* was on the lower Detroit River. The grandeur was then wiped away. Near Bar Point, she touched bottom and opened a gaping hole in her hull. The ship began taking on so much water that her captain had the flag of distress raised, the inverted stars and stripes of the American flag. Her predicament was sighted by the officers of a ship named for a city thematic of Americanism and all things red, white, and blue, *Philadelphia.* The *Philadelphia* intercepted a tug, which was sent to assist the *RW&B.* That meant another trip to the drydock, but the bark sailed on.

Scrolling through newspaper microfilms from this period offers a titillating portal into the past, illuminating the broad range and contents the daily newspaper provided readers. There was a flair for sensationalism and jarring, sometimes ghastly, headlines. Newspapers embodied the entire pantheon of media. There were, in addition to world and national news, social commentary and content; entertainment features, travelogues, eclectic features, and far-flung stories from across the globe and down the street, and even novellas. The marine news columnist positions on the dailies of major port cities along the lakes were plum posts. The journalists tending these columns often shared information, so that crossover news reports were common. News and features of local interest prevailed, and frequently there would be lengthy screeds and epistles. It was also the era of no bylines, making it extremely difficult or impossible to name the columnists.

In the 1870s and 1880s, the port of Chicago would frequently see daily arrivals and departures numbering well over one hundred vessels, most of which were schooners. In these crowded harbor scenes, teeming with the din of industry, factory whistles blew in discordance with steamboats. Schooners and steamers and tugboats would stage and jockey and nudge and fight for dock space and open lanes into and out the river. Even in the open water of the lakes, congestion near, and sometimes afar, made sailing a tricky proposition. Thus, the *RW&B*'s frequency of finding another craft to collide with is understandable.

On October 8, 1873, while upbound on lower Lake Huron, the inveterate *RW&B* collided with the schooner *Guiding Star*—yet another ironic and inappropriately named vessel to smack into. The bark lost her jibboom, bowsprit, and headgear;

the *Guiding Star* suffered a damaged rail and bulwarks. Both made their way back to Port Huron shipyards for repairs.

Whether for economic reasons pinned to the bleak period of years following the Panic of 1873 or other events in the time, or simply by favorable luck for a change, things were quiet in the operations of the boat for a spell. Five years would elapse before the *RW&B* earned noteworthy ink again.

In a roundup of activities on Lake Michigan published in the *Chicago Inter-Ocean* on November 7, 1878, highlighting several days of mishaps and misfortunes and weather-related muggings, the *RW&B* made a paragraph: "The bark Red, White and Blue and brig Waucoma lost light spars on the lake [Michigan] last week—the former one of her topsail yards, and the latter her fore-yard. The canvas of both vessels also suffered damage."

Two words from this missive, "topsail yards," channel us into the next phase of life for the *RW&B*. During a winter lay-up of 1878–1879, likely at Milwaukee, the ship underwent a change in her rigging. A bark when she hunkered down for the cold, she was converted to the more conventional fore-and-aft schooner outfit. According to documents issued by the Milwaukee Customs House, she was still owned by Fitzgerald concerns, if not the Fitzgerald brothers, in 1879, Fitzgerald and Company. She was valued at $14,000 and tagged with a B-1 rating. *RW&B* would see her ratings read like bottles of multiple vitamins in a medicine cabinet over her career—A-1, A-2, B-1, A-2½—and shuffled like a deck of playing cards from the beginning to the end of her life.

Any optimistic expectations that the "new" *RW&B*, having joined the ranks as a schooner, would have a less contested future were damped before 1879 was peeled from the calendar. In a floating column headline worthy of Elizabeth Barrett Browning, "Tidings over the wires," this special telegram was sent to the *Chicago Inter-Ocean:* "Milwaukee, Wis., Nov. 28—This afternoon the vessel Red, White and Blue, coal-laden, collided with the Huron Street bridge while in tow of the tug Maxon, by which part of her rigging and gear was torn off, and a hole was torn in her cabin. The bridge was also considerably damaged."

When the propeller *St. Paul* reached Detroit on August 22, 1881, her officers reported seeing a three-mast schooner loaded and aground on Pelee Island of Lake Erie. The sighting was corroborated by the crew of the steamer *Morley.* A Canadian tug was dispatched, and later, yet another of those ornate wooden wonders of tugboats, this time the *Winslow.* Of course, the grounded schooner was the *RW&B.* The *Winslow* tugged at her and was later joined in the effort by a vessel identified as the tug *Bob Hackett.* After forty tons of the *RW&B*'s coal cargo was lightered, she floated free, pleasantly undamaged.

Early in the 1882 shipping season, the *RW&B* departed Chicago with a cargo of corn, set for delivery to an undisclosed location, quite likely Buffalo. When she arrived at Port Huron she was found to be leaking. A considerable portion of her cargo was saturated. This misfortune would provide a brief vignette, a quick peek of behind the scenes operations of insuring payloads and the principals involved in managing the schooner. When a telegram was received at Chicago detailing the boat's dilemma, the insurers of the corn, the interests and underwriters of the Chicago Grain Insurance Pool, moved quickly. They dispatched a man whose name rolled like a toboggan run, Captain Cal Carr, to Port Huron to inspect the ship and damaged cargo.

On the return to Chicago following the wet corn episode, there was another testament to the whims and vicissitudes in the lot of sailing ships plying the lakes. Unlike the *RW&B*'s swift voyage from Buffalo to Port Huron in the span of three days in 1868, this backtrack to Chicago was punctuated by torpid weather conditions. She only made it as far as Milwaukee. On May 24, crewmen launched her yawl and rowed into harbor. Her provisions had been exhausted on her unexpectedly long fourteen-day trip from Presque Isle, Pennsylvania, and the boys were hungry.

The *RW&B* sailed late into the 1883 season. When she checked into Chicago for her final trip of the year, the proprietors of the McArthur Company of that city were no doubt a bit chagrinned. The deck load of lumber they anticipated the schooner would deliver didn't materialize along with the boat. The *RW&B* went ashore on Beaver Island in northern Lake Michigan and freed herself by pitching the deck load overboard.

In early August the following summer, she arrived at Chicago with her fore-topmast broken off. It was believed to have been a casualty of a lightning strike sustained when the boat sailed through a thunderstorm on Lake Michigan. It appeared that anything that *could* happen to the *RW&B would.* It could be pointed out that through all of her incidents—lightning strikes, dead calms, collisions, leaks, and groundings—the boat had fared quite well out on the lake under the tests of heavy weather. That would soon change.

After the boat left Buffalo coal-laden for Chicago late at night on October 13, 1886, a full gale built over Lake Erie. The *RW&B* was escorted on this venture, unusual for her. The schooner *Newsboy* was in the tandem tow of the tug *Crusader* along with her. Near Conneaut, their situations grew perilous. The *Newsboy* broke free and set course back to Buffalo. The *RW&B* was untethered at the same time. Now unburdened and rolling and pitching on the tumultuous Lake Erie, the *Crusader* too turned about and made for Buffalo. Captain Shaw held the *RW&B*'s course, but as the wind increased and swung more westerly, he sought to bring his charge under the shelter of Long Point.

By nightfall, with the wind flexing its muscle at its greatest strength, the schooner began suffering from the beating it was subjected to. At around 9:00 p.m., a marauding sea boarded her over the stern, demolishing her steering gear box and unshipping the wheel. The boat was "jumping furiously," and with painstaking difficulty an iron tiller was attached to the rudder post and maneuvered with tackle jury rigged from the side. That soon gave way. Adrift and at the mercy of the wind and seas, she fell into the dreaded trough, rolling violently, continuously.

Shaw reported seas that rolled six to eight feet over the *RW&B*'s sides and one particular rogue that tore his ship's remaining foresail away, "as if it were gauze." Booms, a portion of her bulwarks, canvas, and portable items thrashed her deck. Shaw reported that he and his mate and other seamen were thrown to the deck and under threat of being snuffed out by the seas and projectiles hurling about. "Everyone thought their time had come," Shaw grimly recalled.

Throughout the hellish night they were assaulted by Lake Erie. At 2:00 a.m. the next day, a Friday, Shaw had the boat's anchors dropped. A few hours later, anchors still holding, they were able to ascertain that their position was about five miles from Dunkirk, New York. The ship was leaking; the *RW&B* had about two and a half feet of water in her hold. The crew pumped, and as the storm abated around daybreak, Shaw had the flag raised in distress.

The first vessel to reach the imperiled *RW&B* was the propeller *Arizona*, bound for Erie, Pennsylvania. How the fortunes change. Hours earlier, Shaw had all but consigned his boat and crew to the lakebed, but now he was being selective about aid or rescue. He declined the *Arizona*'s offer of a tow to Erie; he instead wanted Buffalo for the repairs he knew his boat would need. When the *Arizona* reached Erie, her captain related the *RW&B*'s condition, and the revenue steamer *Commodore Perry* went to her aid. The *Perry* towed the harried schooner to Buffalo, ragged, but still strong and proud.

Damage to the *RW&B*—repairs to the rudder casing and a new outfit of canvas, as well as other repairs—ran the bill to $2,200.[2] The schooner departed Buffalo on

---

2. To bring those dollars into context, the eminent historian Richard White, in his 2017 masterpiece of the era, *The Republic For Which It Stands: The United States During Reconstruction and the Gilded Age, 1865–1896*, writes that "In 1880 the per capita income in Michigan was only $183, and was falling."

October 25. By early November she was chartered to run iron ore from Escanaba, Michigan, at a dollar a ton.

Six years later, she got another dose of Lake Erie's oft-wicked temper. From the 1892 *United States Life-Saving Service Annual Report*: "Nov 10. Am. Schooner *RW&B*. Port Marblehead, Lake Erie. Carried away sails, rigging and steering gear in squall; leading and her crew worn out by working pumps. Went out in tow of tug and ran line to schooner; assisted to heave up anchor, manned pumps, and made temporary repairs to steering gear; tug then towed her to place of safety."

Around noon on October 12, 1895, Captain Morrison of the steamer *Simon J. Murphy*, a brand-new, unique, steel-hulled creation on the Great Lakes, reported upon reaching his destination of Menominee, Wisconsin, that he had spotted a steamer and her consort stranded on Whaleback Shoal, in the middle of Green Bay.[3] Morrison noted that the steamer, in endeavoring to free herself, had succeeded in changing her position somewhat while he observed. Neither vessel was flying a distress flag. Winds were calming, as were the seas, which had been whipped along with a driving rain.

If one thing can be agreed upon in reports filtering in from across various ports along the upper lakes at the time of this incident, it would be that the wind was out of the north, or at one northerly quadrant. At Port Huron, for instance, some thirty vessels returned to port or anchorage on the St. Clair River to escape the howling northeast winds and building seas. They ranged in shape and size and build, from wood to composite to iron: vessels that would one day founder in one Great Lake or another, including the *Churchill*, *John Owen*, and *Russia*.

The steamer that Morrison sighted from the bridge of the *Murphy* proved to be the *Otego*, which did in fact work itself free and thump into Green Bay. The companion that remained in the clutches of the shoal was the *RW&B*. The *Otego*, with Captain Joseph Doville, and the *RW&B*, by this time owned in Lorain, Ohio, with Captain Dan Titus, were coal-laden on a run from Toledo to Green Bay when the whaleback intervened.

The *RW&B* finally reached the end of the line. Captain Titus sent a telegram to his friend, Captain C. E. Benham, from Escanaba on October 18: "Went to the vessel this morning with a tug, pump and lighter. Northwest gale of yesterday used her up. Deck all gone from the mainmast to the cabin and her keel box is pushed up. Think she is broken in two and will abandon her."

---

3. If Green Bay were a football field, Whaleback Shoal might be the fifty-yard line, where a team would paint its logo. It rises like an obscene gesture, close to breaking the water surface, surrounded by deep water.

In researching the *RW&B* so many years ago, amid all the scrapes with disaster and destruction, I couldn't find a case of a single loss of life attached to her. In remembrance of the durable and adventuresome bark-turned-schooner, it would be appropriate to raise a toast in her memory.

The *Eastland* Sets Sail

It was clear from the outset that domineering, alpha males were goading their counterparts at competing South Haven, Michigan, steamboat operations. These were the halcyon days of the lucrative passenger and excursion trade on the Great Lakes, in the early, promising twentieth century. The Dunkley–Williams line had just placed an order for a boat with the Craig Shipbuilding Company of Toledo, Ohio, and the Michigan Steamship Company had done the same with the Jenks Shipbuilding Company at Port Huron, Michigan.

Both wanted the rich interior furnishings the era could offer to appoint their boats, and not only wanted speed to outpace each other, but both wanted the same name: *City of South Haven.* Although testy, the principals of both sides proved that the art of compromise could also be reached. They entered agreement that the first boat to be launched would be awarded the naming right; the other line would hold a contest open to the public and the winning name would be chosen by the shareholders and trustees. Thus, by December 1, 1902, the first race these steamers would be involved in—the race to completion—was underway. The winter ahead would bring the songs of industry and the din of hammered steel at work over the Maumee and Black Rivers. Thus, it fell into the lap of the Michigan

Steamship Company to open the contest of naming its new steamer when the Craig yard launched first, securing for Dunkley–Williams the eponymous *City of South Haven* right.

At the time when the *Eastland* was launched at the Jenks works on May 6, 1903, Della Reid was being presented with a ten-dollar bill and a pass on the new steamer, her prizes for winning the naming contest. Her winning entry was selected from thousands that poured in from around the nation. As luck would have it, Reid resided in South Haven, Michigan, a fortuitous coincidence.

The attendant celebration at Port Huron could be anticipated. Depending on sources, many hundreds or many thousands were on hand to witness the *Eastland*'s launch that day. The honor of christening went to Frances Pereue. Her husband and a vital cog in the machinations of the Michigan Steamship Company, John Pereue, would be the *Eastland*'s captain. Whistles across the city were blown as the new steamer dipped into the Black River. The Jenks Shipbuilding Company was closed for the day in order to permit the workers who had toiled on the *Eastland* to witness their hard work take float.

The *Eastland* was the first passenger boat to be built at Port Huron since twenty years earlier, when the ferry steamer *Omar D. Conger* was launched. In fact, the *Conger* was on the Black River that very day, unintentional though her presence was. She was being prepped for some sprucing up to welcome the new season, including a new coat of paint.[1]

For me, and I suspect anyone who has viewed the photographs of that nightmare horror-show day on the Chicago River in 1915, the images of the overturned *Eastland* and the recovery of the bodies of the victims, the rows and rows of bodies in the makeshift morgues, are forever seared into one's memory. But for a moment, harken back to the night of July 15, 1903, as the *Eastland* is set to depart on her maiden voyage.

At the foot of Griswold Street, where the Black River flows into the rambunctious St. Clair River, the boat was docked. The public was invited aboard to tour the proud creation of its city's laborers. Entering at the main deck and passing the passenger lobby, people may have found it unimpressive, as much space here was devoted to freight. On the second deck, however, things gained elegance. First-class

1. On March 26, 1922, docked along this same Black River at Port Huron, the *Conger* suffered a mysterious and deadly explosion. The boat was reduced to kindling, and windows up to four blocks away were shattered. Four were killed in the *Conger* explosion, including one of her firemen, whose body was reportedly found atop a nearby coal pile.

passenger accommodations ran along the sides of the deck, and it also housed the main salon. The dining room, too, was on this deck. A dumbwaiter brought dishes up from below decks, where the galley was hidden from view.

Still more first-class cabins ran the entire length of the third deck, and a promenade looped around the entire boat. Aft on this deck was the *Eastland*'s smoking room, running the width of the steamer. The fourth deck was the fully exposed promenade deck; here lifeboats, skylights, the twin smokestacks and anchoring wires and cables were fixed. The *Eastland* was outfitted with one hundred first-class staterooms. Creature comforts provided were bath and running water, electric lights, and rich mahogany woodwork. All other staterooms were finished in white and gold décor. The smoking room was appointed in leather and oak. Red carpeting was used throughout the boat.

That glistening summer night at the foot of Griswold Street, the *Eastland* was illuminated by all 950 of her electric lights, a magnificent, shimmering testament to the art of shipbuilding. Her spotlight was used to pierce the night sky and friskily dance over Port Huron and the St. Clair River. When the *Eastland* departed at 2:30 a.m. on the sixteenth, the bevy of shareholders, backers, guests, and local dignitaries aboard had finally gone to bed. One may assume that they slept soundly, but nights of sleeplessness were just ahead for the *Eastland*'s charges. The next several weeks for the nascent steamer and her headstrong ownership were going to be challenging. Before a triad of misfortune would begin hounding the boat that summer, there was a prevailing business matter that overarched both the *Eastland*'s ownership group and the shipbuilder.

Agreeing upon a guaranteed speed of twenty miles per hour for the new steamer, the Michigan Steamship Company sweetened its agreement with the Jenks Shipbuilding Company. Along the lines of incentive clauses stitched into the contracts of some modern day athletes, the Michigan Steamship Company obliged to pay the Jenks concerns an additional $2,500 for each quarter mile per hour the *Eastland* attained in speed, up to twenty-two miles per hour, the apex of desire. The *Eastland*'s owners had no problem with adding an additional $20,000 to the Port Huron shipbuilders. The watershed mark was the mutually accepted twenty miles per hour Bound to that mark of speed, the Jenks Shipbuilding Company would shave the same $2,500 per quarter mile per hour if the steamer failed to meet the guaranteed speed.

It took no time at all for the anticipated rivalry between the *Eastland* and the *City of South Haven* to commence, in proving which steamer was fleetest. To the victor would come the boasting rights as the reigning queen of Lake Michigan speedsters. On July 26, the first unofficial race was run. Newspaper accounts called it a draw. William Jenks did not. A tacit man in business concerns, he said frankly, "The *Eastland* made the trip between South Haven and Chicago in much less time than the other boat ever made it . . . it will continue to increase in speed." Observers demurred, claiming the race took four hours, fifteen minutes, no improvement over the normal running time, indicating the *Eastland* was short of the speed guaranteed by the Jenks Shipbuilding Company interests.

This set the stage for the coming weeks of the *Eastland*'s entrance into service. Already, regardless of what her speed might be, the steamship was coming under attack by various unions. Initially, fingers were pointed at the Jenks Shipbuilding Company, purportedly a non-union entity. In the first staged race, just described, both steamers carried double crews in the engine room to keep steam high. Black gang members on the *Eastland* were quick to stage a loud protest, claiming the company reneged on paying the promised wage, raising the ire of many.

Right around this same time, after apparently striking some unseen underwater obstruction, damaging one of her screws, the *Eastland* limped into Chicago. Due at 10:00 p.m., the boat clunked to her dock at 1:00 a.m., her excursionists reportedly "tired-out and disgusted." After the passengers disembarked, the *Eastland* moved downstream on the Chicago River. Near the junction of the river's north branch, above the Wells Street bridge, the *Eastland* clipped the tug *George K. Gardner.* Receiving this glancing blow rolled the tug, filling her hold and engine room with water, sinking it on the spot. "All that can be seen of the tug is her smokestack and pilothouse, which protrude above water," the newspaper account read.

Then came the "potato mutiny" in mid August. At face value, the episode was both folly and bizarre, but yielded serious consequences. As it went, six of the *Eastland*'s firemen abruptly stopped working as the steamer was mid-lake on a scheduled run. They carped that they weren't served potatoes with their meal. The effects of their actions were immediate: the steamer slowed to a crawl. Some reports said that Pereue restrained and detained the wildcat strikers with a pistol in hand and the aid of a Chicago policeman who happened to be along on the trip,. When the boat arrived in South Haven, authorities led them away in manacles to jail cells. Dangling charges of mutiny hung over their heads soon thereafter, absurd as it seems.

David McKiffin, the Business Agent for the firemen's union, called a strike against the *Eastland.* It lasted all of ten hours. The Lake Carriers Association at

Buffalo intervened and informed McKiffin that his wildcat was null and void. The *Eastland* was enrolled with the Lake Carriers Association and protected by the season's contract with the firemen's union. The whole sticky, silly mess was eventually resolved, but by now it was clear that the unguent in need of application was one for union unrest, not for buttery mashed potatoes.

Tugboats began a blacklist of the *Eastland* then, if briefly. When Pereue signaled for a tug upon arrival at the South Haven pierheads, none came. This was further evidence of the disdain for the *Eastland* in her early going. Pereue was undeterred and nosed the boat to her dock unassisted.

Indications were mounting that the *Eastland* was not making the twenty miles per hour promised by the Jenks Shipbuilding Company, perhaps reaching the Dunkley–Williams folks. On August 8, just ahead of the potato mutiny, Dunkley–Williams announced to the press that it would accept a speed challenge from the Michigan Steamship Company, pitting its *City of South Haven* against the *Eastland.* Its acceptance said, in large part, "The public offer of the Michigan Steamship Company to wager $1,000, $5,000 or any amount they may see fit to place that their boat can out run the steamship *City of South Haven* we shall be glad to accept, and will cover any amount they see fit to put up . . . the only provision we insist upon is that there shall be no passengers aboard, and we would also desire that the winning company donate the money to some charitable organization."

Despite the gauntlet thrown at its feet, the Michigan Steamship Company would not defend its steamer. Not in this year of 1903, anyway. What perturbed the cranky *Eastland* remained uncertain. On August 29, the Jenks Shipbuilding Company announced that the scheduled official testing of the *Eastland*'s speed had been aborted. Difficulties hobbling the *Eastland,* at least those reported in the press, centered around a wire cable that had worked its way via one of her propellers to be ground into some bearings. With the *Eastland* dispatched to a drydock on the north branch of the Chicago River again, the Michigan Steamship Company chartered the steamer *Soo City* to fill her absence.

Two days later, another shoe fell heavily, like a work boot. The Michigan Steamship Company announced that Pereue had resigned his position of captain of the *Eastland.* Forced to read tea leaves through the gauzy veil of history, one can easily lean toward believing that Pereue, a key figure in the fledgling steamship line, wouldn't voluntarily quit a post dear to him. It would be easier to conclude that Pereue was forced out, from the fact of the *Eastland*'s recent entry into service, right down to his wife being chosen to christen the boat less than four months earlier.

On September 1, Captain Frank Dority was announced as Pereue's successor. Dority came from another storied Lake Michigan passenger boat operation, the Goodrich Transit Company, where he had charge of their steamer *Georgia.* Hiring Dority was allegedly for the experience he could bring to mitigate the *Eastland*'s untapped speed, as he was familiar with and had sailed twin screw steamers.[2] By all indications the *Eastland* didn't return to service on Lake Michigan. In fact, on the afternoon of September 22 she was back in Port Huron, at the foot of Griswold Street. It was no victory lap.

The booming Jenks Shipbuilding Company was toiling away at other projects. The big steel freighter *F. B. Squire* was slated to be launched that autumn, and full attention was being paid to getting the *Squire* afloat. Two months later, the *Eastland* remained at the foot of Griswold. The curiosity of the marine beat reporter must have gotten the better of him, so that he inquired at the Jenks Shipbuilding Company yard about the *Eastland*'s status. He would report, succinctly, that the steamer would "have her machinery overhauled and improved over the winter."

It appears that the Jenks Shipbuilding Company guarantee of twenty miles per hour to the *Eastland* fell short. It seems fair to connect the dots to this, at least. William Jenks wasn't talking; we can only surmise. There is one indisputable takeaway: hundreds of thousands had come to wish that the *Eastland* had never returned to Lake Michigan.

2. When the steamer *Soo City*, the *Eastland*'s replacement as noted in this article, was later sold off-lakes in 1908 to Texan Felix Jackson for intended use between New Orleans and various Texas ports, Frank Dority was hired to sail the *Soo City* as captain. The *Soo City* never made it, disappearing in the Gulf of St. Lawrence during a howling blow, claiming the lives of Dority and eighteen others.

The Coming of the Yellow Monster

In recent shipping seasons, various ports along the Great Lakes have played host to a garish trio of Netherlands-flagged heavy lift ships. They sail with the name prefix "Happy"—*Happy River*, *Happy Ranger*, and *Happy Rover*. They are a joyous sight to behold: the hull color is bold yellow, quite a rare feature. Not all show by any means, one of the Happy family, the *Happy Rover*, in 2016 became the first heavy lift vessel ever to sail the North Seas route and Northwest Passage within one season, and the first to use the Fury and Hecla Strait between the Pacific and Atlantic Ocean. The sight of the mirthful Happies visiting the lakes recalls the 1904 launching at Lorain, Ohio, of the *Augustus B. Wolvin*. When the *Wolvin* entered service and during her first years of operation, she too sported the uncommon yellow hull scheme. A version of this story originally appeared in *Telescope*, the defunct journal of the Great Lake Maritime Institute, in the November–December 1991 edition.

The Bay of Biscay is an acute wedge of the Atlantic Ocean that cleaves and defines the borders of France and Spain. Inland, the Pyrenees Mountains run along these same geographic configurations. An area rich in agriculture and livestock, it is also rich in seafaring traditions of the French and Spanish fleets that sailed these waters for centuries. Not far from the French border in Spain, where the Pyrenees fall to the foothills and then to the seashore, is the city of Santander. In addition to the agrarian and livestock economy offered there, the city was also the host to a shipbreaking yard. Outside of the U.S. and Canadian ports and until recent years the emergence of Aliaga, Turkey, as a shipbreaking site, there is probably no place on Earth where lake boat memories died as they did in Santander, Spain. During the 1960s and 1970s, many a laker met the scrap torch in this foreign land far removed from fresh water.

On September 24, 1967, when the lake boats *Wolvin* and *Saskadoc* arrived under tow to Santander harbor, it was the final voyage for both steamers as they were nudged into the scrapper's dock. For the *Wolvin*, her last trip couldn't possibly have been in more contrast to her first.

When construction began on the *Wolvin* on December 1, 1903, at Lorain, Ohio, upon order of lake shipping magnate Augustus B. Wolvin of Duluth, the shipbuilders and the entire lakes shipping community knew they were building a Goliath. Building this monolith would be taking place during one of the most savage winters recorded in the Great Lakes region. By the time the *Wolvin* was ready to slide from the ways, some twenty days of work had been lost due to inclement weather, according to the *Cleveland Plain Dealer.*

Far more than the scene of just another launching, Lorain became the epicenter of unbridled enthusiasm as launch day approached. In early April 1904, with the joyous day imminent, community pride in the shipbuilding city exploded. Five thousand invitations were sent out and handbills were posted in cities and towns from Fort Wayne, Indiana, to Erie, Pennsylvania, and as far south as Bridgeport, Ohio, opposite Wheeling, West Virginia. A twenty-five-gun salute was planned for when the *Wolvin* took to the water. A ball was scheduled for that night, with the proceeds to be funneled into the Lorain Public Library for the purchase of new books.

On Saturday April 9, 1904, the population of Lorain swelled by the thousands. The launch day of the *Wolvin* saw a mass of humanity lining the Black River, packing the rooftops of buildings and sheds and workshops, crowding the rails of the steamer *Henry Steinbrenner*, which was tied up opposite the drydock. There was literally no vantage point in Lorain harbor unoccupied. At about one o'clock in the afternoon the wife of James C. Wallace (her first name was not given in the newspaper account), the general manager and vice president of the American Shipbuilding Company who supervised the *Wolvin*'s construction, signaled for the lines to be cut.

Mrs. Augustus B. Wolvin (her first name was likewise omitted) shattered a bottle of champagne on the bow of her husband's namesake boat. As it started down the ways, the stern slid ahead of the bow, but by the time the big steamer struck the water she was nearly on an even keel. Euphoria erupted in Lorain. Both citizens and factory whistles sounded, and the cacophony lasted a full five minutes.

Considering the lengthy list of dignitaries attending the *Wolvin*'s launch, it would be accurate to say that everyone who was anyone in lake shipping, building, and management was present. Some four hundred honored guests were served a luncheon in the shipyard's "VIP" quarters while prominent marine men raised toast and speeches were given.

One man took a roasting amid the frivolity. Referred to as General Richardson or E. M. Richardson, the "general" provided the paint that covered the hull of the *Wolvin*. It wasn't the quality of paint for which Richardson was grilled, it was the color—the *Wolvin* was painted yellow.

The *Wolvin* itself was a marvel. Every so often in the annals of Great Lakes history the word "prototype" is affixed to a vessel for its unique, often-replicated design in the advancement of the industry: trendsetters, not followers. The *Wolvin* was such a trendsetter. At 560 feet in overall length, the *Wolvin* bettered by sixty feet the existing lake boat nearest her length. She was fifty-six feet in her beam and boasted a depth of thirty-two feet. Truly a giant of her time, the boat incorporated many new features that prior to her launch had been untried. Most notable was the construction of her cargo hold, which was built in the form of a hopper. It was of continuous length, stretching 490 feet without division or bulkhead intervention, measuring forty-three feet at the top and twenty-four at the bottom. The space between the *Wolvin*'s keel and its hopper was used for water ballast and ran up the height of her main deck stringer.

She had thirty-three hatches on her spar deck, measuring thirty-three by nine feet each, spaced on twelve-foot centers. Her hatch covers had steel plate sidings, and with the use of a steam engine, there was virtually no physical labor involved in opening and closing them. She had duplicate steam plants, in the event of failure, not only for this exercise but for lights, windlass, and capstan. The *Wolvin* was flush decked, with only her low-slung aft quarters, pilot house, and Texas (more like Rhode Island) deck protruding above her spar deck length. Directly below her Texas were five elaborately furnished staterooms, along with a private galley, dining room, and a "social parlor" and two private toilet rooms to boot.

Sporting a smokestack of narrow diameter, the *Wolvin* resembled a barge more than a steamboat. The vessel was powered by a quadruple expansion mill with cylinders that measured 18½, 28½, 43½, and 66 inches in diameter, each with a 42-inch stroke. Cranking at eighty revolutions per minute, it generated two thousand horsepower. The boilers were twin Babcock and Wilcox fire tube units placed twelve feet apart to fire athwartship with a working pressure of more than 215 pounds. Her builders claimed that only seventeen larger vessels plied the waters of the world at the time of her launch. The steamer was built at the cost of $480,000, and some 750,000 rivets were used in hammering her together. Her speed on the lakes would be between eleven and twelve miles per hour when she entered service for Wolvin's wanly, generically named Acme Steamship Company.

On April 17, the *Cleveland Plain Dealer* ran a column retracting a claim that the *Wolvin* could trade only at Conneaut, Ohio, due to her enormous length. The American Shipbuilding Company asserted that the big boat could indeed trade at all Lake Erie ports except Cleveland. Cleveland had ample docks, but they were upriver on the Cuyahoga and vessels smaller than the *Wolvin* experienced great difficulty reaching them due to the wildly bent river. The drum was being banged for ore docks at the outer harbor of Cleveland. In this same column, the *Wolvin* was given a sobriquet that wandered afield from the nickname claimed by John O. Greenwood in his *Namesakes II.* Greenwood called the *Wolvin* the "Yellow Kid." She may have been tagged the Yellow Kid in Lorain, but at Cleveland she was dubbed the "Yellow Monster."

Fit-out work continued for the next several weeks. On Friday May 20, the *Wolvin* had steam raised in her boilers for the first time and they were thoroughly tested. The *Wolvin* was then slated to be towed to the Baltimore and Ohio Railroad docks downriver in Lorain to load coal for her maiden voyage to Duluth. The railroad hastened to accommodate the massive steamboat, while seeking to set a record-breaking pace for loading.

Other vessels lying at the Baltimore & Ohio Railroad car dump had to be jockeyed about to make room for the *Wolvin* as she was towed under the dumpers. In so doing, the steamer *Robert Fulton* inadvertently backed into the *Wolvin* and carved a gash in her side. No serious damage was incurred by either vessel, but the *Cleveland Plain Dealer* noted that the encounter left "an ugly mark on the big fellow's side."

The *Wolvin*'s first load was dumped aboard on May 25. Rail cars were ushered aboard and dumped at a frenetic pace, sometimes two at a time. While a pace of eighteen cars per hour was maintained, the B&O did break its loading record when it dumped twenty-one cars in one hour. The *Wolvin* topped off at 10,250 tons of coal, an amount unheard of until that day. Despite the massive tonnage figure, James C. Wallace expressed disappointment in the *Wolvin* not breaking the twelve thousand–ton mark. Wallace felt the overall dimensions of the steamer would see the number eclipsed.

Under the command of Captain J. W. Norcross, the *Wolvin* departed Lorain on her maiden voyage on the morning of June 10, 1904, for Duluth. Her compliment of guests included master electricians, mechanics, and a compass adjuster, as well as an engineer from the Babcock and Wilcox boiler works. The following morning the *Wolvin* passed Detroit. Despite the early hour, large crowds reportedly lined the docks to wave their approval and ferries crossing the Detroit River blew whistle blasts in salute of the *Wolvin*. Not far from the city of St. Clair on the St. Clair River, the *Wolvin* dropped her twin eight thousand–pound anchors while repairs were made to her steering gear. With a hierarchy of mechanics aboard, the demons were exorcised in four hours and the *Wolvin* moved on. After divesting her coal cargo, the *Wolvin* chugged ahead to the ore docks at Two Harbors, Minnesota. On June 19, 10,894 tons of iron ore were muscled into the Monster's hold. Drawing 18½ feet of water, the steamer departed Two Harbors and surpassed all ore tonnage numbers ever hauled by a single vessel by an astounding margin.

As fate would have it, when the *Wolvin* locked through at the Soo with her record cargo, she locked down alongside another ore-laden steamer powered by a quadruple expansion engine. It was noted that as the two boats cleared DeTour and began the plodding journey down Lake Huron a race ensued—if it can be considered such a contest between groaning freighters crammed with iron ore. The second vessel was the *Presque Isle*. The lethargic race between the *Wolvin* and the *Presque Isle* would play out in the reach of longevity for the *Presque Isle*. It would go on sailing for well over twenty years after the *Wolvin* met the torch in Santander, then in the bulk cement trade as the much beloved *E. M. Ford* of the Huron Cement fleet.

A couple of years after the *Wolvin* entered service, the first in the six hundred–foot class of ore boats were sailing the lakes and the supernova aura surrounding the *Wolvin* had faded. Years later her forward and aft superstructures were rebuilt and towered over her original lines. To no surprise, the unique yellow hull would be repainted with one of the prevailing color schemes found on lake boats. At Port Huron, Michigan, on June 18, 1909, the marine news reporter for the *Port Huron Daily Times* noted the as the *Wolvin* passed by it was in a state of metamorphosis. "The vessel is being painted a dull red instead of yellow, which color it has carried since being placed into commission a few years ago."

The *Wolvin*'s reign in her original livery was short, but it certainly left lasting impressions on the legion of observers she sailed past in her early years of operation. I have those optics myself when the *Happy River* or *Happy Ranger* passes on the nearby St. Clair River; they may be flagged to another nation but they conjure a memory from the days of yore on the Great Lakes.

The Reluctant Acceptance of Wireless Use on the Great Lakes

In George Hilton's superb book *The Great Lakes Car Ferries*, a single footnote in the text opens doors to questions. Hilton quotes text taken from a 1901 edition of the *Railway and Engineering Review*, stating, "The officials of the Pere Marquette Railway are considering the adoption of wireless telegraphy for their vessels . . . this means of communication is considered superior to the use of carrier pigeons."

How was Guglielmo Marconi's wireless telegraph, or radio, a sensational advancement in communications to humankind, appraised along the Great Lakes? What do we know about its adoption by shippers and vessel operators? And really, carrier pigeons?

Marconi was a young man in Bologna, Italy, in the autumn of 1894, not yet twenty-one years of age. He was fascinated by the recent discovery of the radio wave, then called the "Hertzian wave" in honor of German discoverer Heinrich Hertz. Marconi's fascination with the electrical wave concerned whether it could be harnessed to work in similar fashion to the telegraph, sans, of course, the wiring. His father was encouraging and allotted him space in his garden, where the intrepid Marconi began his experiments. He was soon sending signals over the plots of vegetables and flowers.

As Marconi tinkered, Captain Edwards piloted the steamer *State of Ohio* out of Buffalo on Wednesday night, October 10, 1894. Besides the customary allotment of crew and passengers and mixed freight, Edwards had brought along three carrier pigeons belonging to G. A. Reinhart, presumably a friend of the captain. The *State of Ohio* met with foul weather and was forced to shelter in the lee of Long Point, where it arrived at 12:45 a.m. on the eleventh. After daybreak, Edwards released a pigeon with the following message: "Str. State of Ohio. Long Point. Oct 11, 1894, 7:20 a.m. Arrived here at 12:45 a.m. Wind west, blowing a gale. There are sheltered here the Str. Gratwick, a steel steam barge, with three in tow, and several others. Cap't Edwards." The pigeon arrived back at Buffalo about an hour later, quite an impressive performance turned in by Mr. Reinhart's bird.

Marconi's wireless invention was maturing. By 1899 he had relocated to England. He recognized England as being one of the great shipping nations of the world and sought application of his wireless apparatus where he felt it would best serve with communicating with ships at sea. His wireless was soon transmitting clearly across the English Channel.

Marconi with indomitable spirit dreamed of transmitting a signal that would span the Atlantic Ocean. On December 6, 1901, he arrived at Newfoundland to set up shop. On the twelfth, a mere six days later, he received a dot-and-dash code from England. Transatlantic communication had been achieved; his radio was a smashing success. Marconi's wireless telegraphy was ready for the world, but was the world ready?

In the shipping circles of the Great Lakes, vessel operators, fleet superintendents, ownership groups, insurers, and so forth, the initial reactions would be cool to tepid. The aforementioned Pere Marquette Railway's consideration of Marconi's invention wouldn't bear fruit for several years. Instead, the Detroit & Cleveland Navigation Company's passenger steamer *City of the Straits* is given credit for being the first lake boat to be wireless equipped. The pioneering by the *City of the Straits* in sporting her wireless outfit was hardly magnetic to vessel operators. Additional converts to the new technology were slow to trickle in.

In 1903, a proposal for the use of wireless appeared in the annual report of the United States Life-Saving Service. Each year, the Life-Saving Service formed committees to study and make decisions on improvements. A lifesaver by the name of Sharman (the only name offered in the report) presented to the committee the case for wireless, which consisted of diagrams and results of tests he conducted with the wireless at a radius of two, five, and ten miles. The tests were successes, but in his report he wrote that the success could be achieved "whatever the weather," and those words led to the plan's undoing. In the face of this early science, the skeptics held sway.

In appraisal of the report, the committee concluded that Sharman's statement of "whatever the weather" had contingencies, and Sharman's tests were done only under ideal circumstances. Functioning in turbulent, inconsonant weather conditions wasn't satisfactorily addressed. As a result of this stricture, the Life-Saving Service passed the buck. It suggested that further consideration of the wireless be put to the Lighthouse Board, suggesting, "The Lighthouse Board would be better suited for the adoption of such a system as is here presented, for the reason that lighthouses and lightships are generally placed at prominent points of danger and offer good facilities for establishing the necessary apparatus." The Life-Saving Service never did incorporate wireless equipment. Nor did it concede that its operations were frequently situated near lighthouses in those "prominent points of danger."

Marconi's invention was not always denigrated in the early years. The instrument was achieving worldwide acclaim, even in pockets along the lakes. On May 21, 1905, the Indiana Transportation Company's passenger steamer *Indianapolis* was selected by the government to conduct wireless tests on Lake Michigan. Sixty-one messages were received by the *Indianapolis* as she made the round trip between Chicago and Michigan City, Indiana, including messages to passengers and assignments to newspapermen on the vessel from their office headquarters. The following year, the car ferries of the Ann Arbor Railroad based out of Frankfort (Elberta), Michigan, became the first cross-lake boats to receive Marconi's wondrous invention.

In the spring of 1907, fledgling signs of a new attitude were developing among lake shippers as they began to digest the wireless. Many felt the adoption of wireless by passenger-carrying ships of the lakes was justified for the safety of their human cargoes. Harry Coulby, the great president of the Pittsburgh Steamship Company, did not mince words when he spoke to a correspondent of the *Cleveland Plain Dealer* in March 1907. "The boats of the Pittsburgh Steamship Company are not and never will be equipped with wireless," he declared. The Pittsburgh fleet, according to Coulby, was not at a loss for contacting vessel masters. The issue of safety did not enter the conversation.

Marconi shared the Nobel Prize in physics in 1909 with Karl Ferdinand Braun for their tireless contributions and development in wireless telegraphy. Later that year a disaster on Lake Erie—the disappearance of the car ferry *Marquette & Bessemer*

No. 2 with the loss of all hands, possibly thirty-five souls—provided the impetus for the installation of wireless on the car ferries of the Pere Marquette Railway.

Ten months later, in September 1910, the equipping of the Pere Marquette ferries paid quick dividends. On September 9, the *Pere Marquette 18* foundered on Lake Michigan. Before succumbing to the waves, the *Pere Marquette 18* sent a wireless transmission to which her sister ship, the *Pere Marquette 17*, was able to respond. Despite heavy loss of life, thirty-five people were saved. Had the boats of the Pere Marquette fleet been without wireless, it is feasible the *Pere Marquette 18* would have gone down with no survivors.

The very next month, however, the anti-wireless Coulby would pluck a feather to wear in his hat. In the wee hours of October 2, the steamer *New York* became a victim of tempestuous Lake Huron. The entire crew of the *New York* would be rescued by the Pittsburgh Steamship Company's steamer *Mataafa*, alerted to the *New York*'s plight by distress flares. There remained the tricky issue of getting the *New York*'s people safely transferred from a lifeboat to the *Mataafa*. It was an act of legerdemain to aid in rescue: To quell the upheaval of Lake Huron waves, storm oil was poured over the *Mataafa*'s rail. The action worked, and *Mataafa* Captain Hugh Regan, given credit for the application of the oil essential to the rescue, was lauded by the Pittsburgh Steamship Company. Coulby immediately instructed masters of the Pittsburgh fleet to carry storm oil. For the time being, petroleum products outranked wireless on the Pittsburgh boats.

Coulby had many allies in his disdain of wireless equipped lake freighters, including the prestigious Lake Carriers' Association (LCA). In April 1912, the loss of the *Titanic* on the North Atlantic sent shockwaves rippling through worldwide shipping. By early July of that year a senate committee on commerce began gathering experts and hearing testimonies in Washington, DC, as new bills were being proposed to safeguard the lives of people at sea. On July 9, William Livingstone, president of the LCA, and Harvey Goulder, council for the LCA, sat before the committee. They were informed that A. A. Schantz, vice president and general manager of the Detroit and Cleveland Navigation Company, and representing the lake passenger carriers, had testified that the lake freighters needed the same wireless equipment many of the passenger vessels on the lakes then employed. Livingstone was incensed, and immediately countered by suggesting that passenger boats of the lakes be required to have steel deck construction, pointing to only two such vessels that did not have highly inflammable wooden decks. Livingstone deftly deflected the argument for wireless.

Goulder cited Schantz's recommendation for wireless installation on freighters and asked, "I wonder if he [Schantz] would be ready to bear a part of that expense. We cannot do it out of our freight returns. Instead of needing wireless to summon the vessels to us we are endeavoring now to devise a method to keep them away from us, to avoid collisions. We can summon vessels at any time with rockets or whistles. We do not need wireless."

Marconi continued revamping and improving the wireless. The following year of 1913 would bring to the lakes a double-barreled volley: the Big Storm of 1913, and the initial hearings by the House Committee on Merchant Marine and Fisheries for provisions of the proposed La Follette Seaman's Act.

The Big Storm of 1913, some of the darkest hours of marine history ever on the Great Lakes, needs no recap here. The only wireless-equipped bulk freighters on the lakes at the time were the boats of the Shenango Furnace Company, all of which escaped damage or destruction through forewarning. The stayed snug in port or sought shelter. As news was being reported of the discovery of a capsized, floating hull on Lake Huron, which proved to be the *Charles S. Price*, the steamers of the Shenango fleet were sending off wireless messages detailing to anxious owners the groundings and stranding of numerous vessels. The Department of Commerce later would acknowledge the value of wireless to the Shenango fleet.

In December 1913, vessel owners nationwide congregated in Washington, DC, for the House hearings on the proposed La Follette Seaman's Act. Controversial Robert M. La Follette, the fiery, egalitarian senator from Wisconsin, with the influence of sailor and activist Andrew Furuseth, wrote, sponsored, and pushed this bill, designed to improve the lives of both seamen and the civilian population that sailed the lakes and seas. Vessel operators loathed La Follette's proposed improvements and the reach of the bill. Wireless use was a topic of debate. The La Follette Seaman's Act became law in 1915, sans wireless mandating; this never became language in the bill, eschewed in favor of hard-fought safety and civil matters of shipboard life.

Two days before Christmas in 1913, Captain Edward Smith of the Great Lakes Towing Company announced a contract between his company and the Marconi Wireless Telegraphy Company to equip the famous wrecker *Favorite* with wireless. Previously, the Great Lakes Towing Company had agreed to outfit the *Favorite* with the equipment as soon as a hundred lake boats had been so upgraded. In the aftershock of the Big Storm, the bulk freighter interests were warming to the value of Marconi's magnificent device.

Gradually, piecemeal, more and more lake boats were sporting wireless outfitting. There were still carrier pigeons doing some heavy lifting too. On June 28, 1920, one of them, No. A1, 20, L 8526, lighted on the Interlake Steamship Company's ore boat *J. A. Campbell.* The *Campbell* was forty miles below Thunder Bay Island on Lake Huron in a heavy rainstorm when the bird came calling. It was cared for overnight and released the next day near Belle Isle in the Detroit River. When the incident was reported in the *Detroit Free Press*, both the officers and crewmen of the *Campbell* stated they hoped to learn of the pigeon's safe arrival at its destination.

Still, half a generation after the Big Storm of 1913, no blanket policy of wireless use prevailed. The autumn of 1929 on Lake Michigan, for instance, saw the disappearance of two steamers without trace and with all hands, the *Andaste* and the car ferry *Milwaukee.* Neither carried wireless.

The Remarkable Remnants of the Lost *Sevona*

There is a lengthy list of "firsts" in the annals of Great Lakes maritime history: the first vessel to reach a given overall length, the first vessel to be powered by a given engine design, the largest tonnage cargo carried, and so forth. The *Emily P. Weed*'s "first" may not have the cachet of some of these claims, but it certainly has sustainability. The *Weed* was the first Great Lakes freighter to have a searchlight mounted on her pilothouse roof.

The *Weed*'s implementation of the incandescent instrument would provide her with chances to flaunt her crowning glory immediately. On her maiden voyage past Port Huron, Michigan, as she thrummed into the St. Clair River downbound on the night of Sunday August 3, 1890, Captain Frank Welcome had it blazing. The *Port Huron Daily Times* reported of the impressive display that "The lamps lit up the whole river." Welcome probably was thinking, why not show it off?

The *Weed* went into service in 1890 under the reins of managing owner C. W. Woodruff. The steamer was a product of the resourceful F. W. Wheeler Shipbuilding Company of West Bay City, Michigan. The *Weed* was steel hulled and three hundred feet in length. She was 1,900 net tons, powered by a triple expansion engine. This size made her one of the larger vessels on the lakes. As she plied the lakes, searchlight penetrating the gloom of night or otherwise, Woodruff was understandably proud of the *Weed.*

There are indications in the historical record available that the *Weed* was, if not built specifically for such purpose, offered for charter in the navigation season. Her brief profile sheet in the Historical Collection of the Great Lakes held in Bowling Green State University's fine archives indicates that Woodruff may have entered into some agreement with the Western Transit Company in this regard. No matter what, it didn't take long for the big *Weed* to etch her name into the record books. On September 2, 1890, she steamed into Buffalo with her hold heaped with one hundred thousand bushels of corn, the largest grain cargo ever carried on the lakes.

There emerged a conspicuous competitive by-product of early steel-hulled steamboats taking to the lakes, an unwritten but inherent need to exhibit their speed. This would go on for the next few decades—new boats racing other new boats and sometimes older boats. It seems to have been a sporting time in the wheelhouses and engine rooms, with these steel-hulled marvels showing not only efficiency and the wave of the future but also the unbridled quest for speed in accomplishment.

The *Weed* was being scrutinized, and the confident Woodruff didn't need a spotlight on himself as he narrated the virtues of the *Weed* He made trips on her and carefully noted her accomplishments to those listening. On September 30, 1891, following a 997-mile trip from Buffalo to Duluth,[1] he offered this testimonial:

> I consider it a good run considering the checks we made at Bar Point, Grosse Point, St. Clair canal, besides several times in Lake Huron and the Sault River [*sic*]. The time from Buffalo to Ft. Gratiot light was 24 hours, from Ft. Gratiot to Detour 14 hours and twenty minutes, from Detour to the Sault Canal locks 5 hours and forty minutes. You can see we checked down considerably in the Sault, as we have run that river in 4 hours and forty-five minutes, and I will say that when this record is broken we will do it in less time. The Weed is a much smarter boat then we expected, and I haven't a doubt that we can get 16mph out of her.

Woodruff wasn't selling the *Weed* on the open market, just her cachet if that time came.

On the sweltering humid day of July 16, 1892, as the *Weed* passed downbound at

1. Woodruff may have shaved off a few miles on this trip.

Port Huron, observers likely had no idea that the cargo she was carrying was highly unusual. Not only unusual, but astounding. The two sentences it warranted in the *Port Huron Daily Times* read with such an innocuous lilt that one must allow it to breathe. Unremarkably, it read, "The steamer Emily P Weed passed down yesterday with 2,900 tons of refined copper valued at $600,000. This is said to be the most valuable cargo ever carried on the lakes." One hundred and twenty-eight years later it is still impressive. In fact, this number is mind-numbing. The value of one dollar in 1891 translates to roughly twenty-seven dollars today, making the *Weed*'s cargo valued in today's currency at some sixteen million dollars.

After the 1896 shipping season the *Weed* went on the market. No blandishment on the steamer's behalf was necessary to Erie, Pennsylvania, vessel owner-operator James McBrier. He purchased the boat and over the ensuing winter initiated some minor changes. The boat was renamed *Sevona*, and marine beat reporters were sniffing around. According to the *Port Huron Daily Times*, on February 10, 1897, two of the *Sevona*'s spars were removed and her power was being reduced. "The aim seems to be to make her earnings more satisfactory than they have been," the report read. "Outsiders say that she has always been something of a disappointment in that direction," the report concluded with a bit of chafing. Four days later, whether following a rebuke by a message from McBrier or otherwise, a modified newspaper account made ink, saying, "It is believed that her earnings in the past have not been altogether satisfactory and an effort to reduce her expenses will be made."

Rewording did little to demystify the information released to the marine world circles that midwinter. If indeed her powerplant was undergoing modifications for economic reasons, was it possible it was consuming coal too quickly? Is that even viable? Did it speak to Woodruff's claim back in 1891 that the steamer's speed may have been linked to greater coal consumption and the *Weed*'s diet thinned profit margins? None of this is clear. Perhaps McBrier deduced that slowing the boat and improving fuel consumption could affect his bottom line.

The driving force of technology in Great Lakes transportation in its steamboats was keen at the time of the *Weed*'s launch. The very next year after the *Weed* set the grain cargo record of 1890, the *E. C. Pope* entered service. In 1891 the *Pope* shattered all records by virtue of the cargo hold that her 332-foot length accorded. The *Pope* was then the largest vessel on the lakes.

As McBrier and the *Sevona* awaited the spring of 1897 and the resumption of the shipping season, the advances in ships and their sizes continued to amaze observers and authorities in the marine community. Staying apace with the constant stretching of the new keels to be laid and the price tags attached to them wasn't a viable direction for many independent ship owners. Although lake boats had reached the dazzling length of four hundred feet by then, the market still left plenty in the pantry on which boats like the *Sevona* could dine. Succinctly and with clarity, however, the owners of the smaller boats could see the future.

In 1904 the *Augustus B. Wolvin* took to the waters of the Great Lakes, all 560 feet of her. This set the shipping world on its ear when the "Yellow Monster," a nickname affixed to her because of her unique hull color, entered service. Many more Goliaths were coming. McBrier could no longer overlook the way the *Sevona* had become vastly undersized in the fledgling world of giant steel steamboats. Placing an order for one of these new centurion steamers was beyond his means. What he could and did do was have the *Sevona* lengthened.

Over the winter of 1904–1905 at Buffalo the lengthening took place. By no means was this obligatory. It was remarkable, if not sensational, for the time and for years to follow. The *Sevona*'s fore and aft sections were stitched back together around a prodigious seventy-two-foot midsection fabrication that nearly tripled her length. Like an early twentieth-century call for a stretch limo, the *Sevona* went from 300 to 372 feet in length in a matter of months. This greatly altered her profile, tonnage, and future.

Entering service as a longer length competitor in the bulk trades of 1905 had by all indications had met McBrier's expectations. The boat's captain, Donald S. McDonald, had been in charge of the boat since McBrier's purchasing it and the renaming, and would now be in charge of an all-new *Sevona* for his ninth year of command. It would become obvious that the stretched *Sevona*'s performance was salutary, and invitations to guests were extended to share in the triumph of her new configuration with cause for proud celebration.

There were guests on board when the *Sevona* pulled away from the Allouez ore docks at Superior, Wisconsin, on the evening of September 1, 1905. She was bound for a Lake Erie with another ore cargo. The term may not have been in place at that time, but the national holiday was, so essentially it was the Friday of the Labor Day Weekend. Perhaps not surprisingly, the weather was foul when the steamer nosed the steamer away from the lakehead.

The weather precipitously went from foul to concerning to dangerous. Winds originating from the southeast swung to a northeasterly direction and increased in velocity. What was in store for the *Sevona* in her plight would be shared with a number of other vessels on Lake Superior in the quickly mounting storm. Winds rose to forty-two miles per hour later that first of September, and gusts of sixty miles per hour were reported. In the late-summer gale, there would be no tales of blinding snow or gathering ice or subfreezing temperatures that so often accompanied Lake Superior shipwreck tales, but shipwrecks and loss of life favor no temperature. In the darkness of Saturday morning the *Sevona* was just east of the Apostle Islands group. McDonald concluded that the punishment his boat was taking was unsustainable, and he made the decision to put about and seek the sheltered waters of the archipelago.

There are several lighthouses scattered among the Apostle Islands group. In a compact distance of some thirty miles there are lighthouses on Sand, Raspberry, Outer, and Devil's islands. A more pertinent or concise example cannot be found as to why all lighthouses on the Great Lakes have different colored lights and flash sequences: why all lights don't flash a white light at thirty-second intervals, for example. No matter what the atmospheric conditions, with or without a searchlight,[2] great seas were running, and with McDonald seeking refuge in the islands, fixing exactly on which lights they would spot was fundamental to his boat and her people's well-being. When the Sand Island light was discerned and the *Sevona* was where he least wanted her to be, his reckoning with this situation of being in the wrong place in the worst of conditions was similar to that felt in many other places on Lake Superior on many other boats.

Reports state that the blow lasted a full twenty-four hours, all through Saturday the second. Wind at Mackinaw City logged at forty-plus miles per hour from the southeast would transform to a northwesterly flow of sustained wind speeds at similar speeds, with higher gusts on western Lake Superior. Those strong northerly winds built harrowing seas. For the people and boats out on Lake Superior at the waning of that summer day, the collateral effects of the roiling lake were stunning. A bitter fate was in store for the *Sevona* in the early hours of Saturday morning the second of September, when she struck and lodged on Sand Island Shoal; had the impact to the boat been as little as fifty feet in any direction—two-thirds the length of her new midbody—the disaster would have been averted. The *Sevona* pinned the tail accurately on the donkey of destruction.

Nothing is known of the final hours of the steamer *Iosco* and her schooner/barge tow, the *Olive Jeanette*, except that they disappeared with all hands, comprising some

2. The records make no mention of the patent device in use before destiny intervened.

twenty-six souls between them. The surviving narrative of other sailors from the harrowing storm can tell us what the crews of the *Iosco* and *Olive Jeanette* could not.

The whaleback steamer *Samuel Mather* suffered greatly on Lake Superior that day. One crewman, his name given as John Lindquist, was swept overboard and lost off Knife Island. A report alluding to this stated that Lindquist, a Swede, had shipped on the *Mather* at Cleveland, and left a wife and family behind in Sweden. Imagine the difficulty of translation to Lindquist's widow when delivering the nightmarish news. It is easy to imagine her saying, "Help me understand this: My husband was the only person lost from this strange ship called a whaleback during a summer storm on a lake and his body can never be recovered?" History would later prove unkind to the *Mather* as well. Renamed *Clifton*, it would disappear on Lake Huron, claiming all hands, on another September day nineteen years into the future.

Irony would come in this blow too. The steamer *North Wind*, of the Mutual Steamship Company, with Captain Thomas Stevenson, steel hulled and similar in size to the *Sevona*, was overwhelmed by the northwest winds and dashed against the south wall of the Duluth ship canal. She sustained a twelve-foot hole in the encounter, sinking immediately in twenty-plus feet of water. Her crew was safe, but ironically, two months into the future another steamer would have a date with destiny on the ship canal at Duluth, this time at the north wall. That would be the fabled *Mataafa*. The uncanniness of these overlapping histories at Duluth and western Lake Superior in 1905 makes a striking comparison, and the actors in the *Sevona*'s plight would curiously mirror that of those in the *Mataafa*, as their episodes played out.

Lindquist's sad loss from the whaleback should have been enough from the "washed overboard" category, but it wasn't. Second engineer Fred Smith of Algonac, Michigan, suffered the same fate some sixty miles east of Keweenaw Point, from the steamer *R. L. Ireland*.

There was a brand new boat on Lake Superior that Saturday, too, one destined for another sixty years of service, the big and bold *Powell Stackhouse.* A product of the Detroit Shipbuilding Company's Wyandotte, Michigan, yard and under the command of veteran Captain Millen, the *Stackhouse* was baptized in the oft-troublesome Great Lakes waters. Millen declared that the big steamer was under constant assault, that hundreds of tons of water washed her decks with regularity. Worse, the patent hatches on the *Stackhouse* kept springing open, allowing frightening amounts of water to enter and inundate her ore cargo. When the *Stackhouse* reached Detroit after the pummeling and the issue of the hatch covers was addressed, Millen said the boat had weathered the blow in good shape. An unidentified crewman, however, felt that if the *Stackhouse* had been out for four or five hours more they would have been in trouble.

When the *Sevona* contacted the shoal off Sand Island that Saturday morning, the impact was severe. Aground and pounding, the forward section began to separate from the midsection. After perhaps half an hour the yawning gap in the hull widened into a ragged steel chasm. In the forward section along with Captain McDonald were two mates, wheelsmen, and watchmen. The stark reality of their situation was chilling: they had no lifeboat.

Probably employing a megaphone, as asserted by Bowen, McDonald relayed instructions to the aft crew. Two lifeboats remained on the aft end of the *Sevona* (one may have already been lost) and the one on the windward side was in a treacherous perch; launching it from where it was held in the davits was a futile proposition. Second engineer Adam Fiden gathered the necessary hands to remove obstacles and stack stays and maneuvered the boat to the leeward side.

As the forward crew did their best to fashion makeshift rafts and flotation devices from hatch covers, chief engineer William Phillipi had the whistle cord of the steamer tied down and the bell chamber blew uninterrupted. It was bellowing until the *Sevona* lost steam, and in the mournful hell unleashed it not only cut any attempt at further commentary between McDonald and the aft crew, but must have been brain-rattling and unnerving. Those on board then retreated to the cabins to wait things out as long and as calmly as they could, insane as it sounds. It wouldn't be long.

One of the aft-end survivors and passengers, Kate Spencer, would be interviewed following the incredible escape from the *Sevona* and subsequent rescue. Her timeline memory differs from Bowen's account of the lifeboats. She recalled, "We were awakened early Saturday morning by Captain McDonald, who told us he was going to run for shelter and that we should secure all breakable stuff as it would toss badly." She specified the disaster's time: "At exactly 5:45 the *Sevona* struck with a terrible crash that threw everybody to the deck. It seemed to us that with the first crash the vessel broke in two." She was further quoted, "The crew told us the break took place where new parts were put in some time ago."

Spencer's account does square with Bowen's inasmuch as abandoning the stricken steamer was for the moment held in abeyance. The inevitable came about five hours later. "At eleven o'clock everything seemed going at once and eleven of us were put in the lifeboat, but as we were pushing off, the five men who were astern called out, 'for God's sake, don't leave us!' so two of our crew helped them get the port boat to the starboard side so they could launch it," Spencer said. This is most likely the instance where Fiden and at least one other repositioned the windward boat to the lee, making its getaway possible.

Against seemingly insuperable odds the occupants of both lifeboats survived. It took more than five harrowing hours before Spencer's lifeboat found the beach on the mainland of Little Sand Bay. The second group in the smaller boat, the ones that pleaded not to be forsaken, was later retrieved by the crew of the tug *R. W. Currie.*

Precisely when the *Sevona* completely succumbed and the forward section disappeared below the surface of the lake is unknown. None of the forward crew of seven survived. The *Currie* would recover the bodies of Captain McDonald and three others. McBrier arrived at Ashland, Wisconsin, a couple of days later, arranging for the transportation of the bodies back to their respective hometowns. The survivors were given passage on the Northwestern railroad to Chicago and personal intermediate points to get them home.

Predictably, the *Sevona*'s lengthening stirred attention and circumspection in the marine circle about the Great Lakes. The prodigious midsection added over the previous winter could hardly merit otherwise. At Detroit, the marine news reporter (and the newspaper from which the accounts from Spencer were taken) caught up to the sage of marine architecture and engineering, Frank E. Kirby. He asked Kirby about the practice and relevance of the lengthening of boats, and whether, following the *Sevona* disaster, this operation should be suspended. Kirby responded, "I myself don't think there is any reason why it should. If a boat is lengthened and the new center is properly tapered toward the bow and the stern, the boat should be as staunch as if entirely new. If this is not done, then there will be trouble, on the theory that a chain is no stronger than its weakest link."

Harkening back to the *North Wind* ripping a gaping hole in herself on the south arm of the Duluth ship canal that September second as the *Sevona* fractured and split on the shoal off Sand Island, the historic inversion of western Lake Superior shipwrecks of 1905 is stark. Although the entire forward crew of the *Sevona* would be lost that September, in late November the steamer *Mataafa* would mortally wound herself in a hellish storm, dashed against the north wall of the Duluth ship canal. Driven north of the wall and broken near the beach in a freezing maelstrom, the forward crew of the *Mataafa* would survive while her entire aft-end crew would freeze to death, as rescue efforts failed.

As wreckage from the *Sevona* reached the beach on Sand Island, including the doomed steamer's wooden hatch covers, a visiting summer resident of the island gathered them. He later lit upon an idea. His name was Sam Fifield, and he was a former lieutenant-governor of the state of Wisconsin. His actions would have lasting impact.

Though the ship had slipped beneath the surface of the water, and thus out of sight forever, the summer of 1908 still evoked thoughts of the lost *Sevona* and would see the final chapter of her saga written in the interest of shipping concerns and a government agency on the lakes. The *Detroit Free Press* reported on June 4 of that year that action was being taken, outlining a letter from Graham D. Fitch, U.S. engineer at Duluth. While reporting on the various depths of water over the *Sevona*'s remains and filing his report, he concluded, "The owner having failed to remove the wreck, action will be taken by the Duluth Engineer office."

Fishermen had stationed buoys over the wreck, one red and one white, and both were still in place when Sarnia, Ontario, wrecker Thomas Reid was contracted to dispatch the remains of the *Sevona*. Reid arrived at Sand Island late on June 11, in command of his tug *Ottawa* and wrecking outfit. Reid reportedly salvaged what he could—boilers and engine—but raising the broken steamer was beyond hope. The hulk was dynamited after cherry-picking the submerged salvage still yielded by the sunken *Sevona*.

Today, one of the *Sevona*'s anchors can be found propped in position on the beach at Little Sand Bay, where it overlooks the steamer's grave, about a mile and a half out. The boat's capstan cover was later salvaged and is now part of the museum collection at the Apostles. It is a gorgeous artifact of Great Lakes marine history, inscribed with the boat's maiden name of *Weed* and her birthplace of West Bay City, Michigan, at the F. W. Wheeler Shipbuilding Company.

There may be one other testimonial to the ship surpassing even the grandeur of the *Weed* capstan cover. When former lieutenant-governor Fifield went about collecting the flotsam from the wrecked *Sevona* just after her demise, including those hatch covers, Fifield had a singular purpose in mind: with these and additional materials, he constructed what was to become the Sevona Memorial Cottage. To the benefit of all, it still valiantly stands on Sand Island, and is on the National Register and State Register of Historic Places.

Hard Bark Harry May and the Mournful *Arcadia*

For a trio of men intent on a nefarious late-night robbery of the master of a vintage schooner docked on Saginaw Bay in Michigan, their intention proved to be ill-conceived. A robber brandishing a pistol would make most sane folks yield to better sense over heroics; maybe you would be left with your life after your money has been fleeced. These three, however, boarded the schooner *Transport* and entered the cabin of the ship's captain, Harry May. As May rose from his bunk to face the perpetrators, he chose a course of action most of us would not. He lowered his head and charged the gun handler, butting him in the gut and sending him reeling. After May yelled for help and alerted his crew, the bandits fled. May retained his money, and probably taught a lesson. Even if this were the only example from which to draw a conclusion about May's brazen, audacious character, it would offer a meaty profile of the man. But this incident in November 1886 is only the beginning of the story.

Long before May could be wed eternally to the diminutive steam barge *Arcadia*, the boat's namesake town had a story worth recounting. An introduction to the village of Arcadia begins with its founder, Henry Starkey. An immigrant from Germany, Starkey settled first in Milwaukee to labor, before crossing Lake Michigan and staking claim to the picturesque site north of Manistee, Michigan.

With boundless energy, Starkey first erected a sawmill on Arcadia Lake that would serve as a shipping point later. Then, sans government assistance, he carved a channel to connect his village with Lake Michigan and developed a small harbor. He built rail lines to link the sapling town to the Toledo and Ann Arbor Railroad. When rumblings began to refer to the bustling town site as "Starkeyville," they were squelched, not only by nearby homesteaders but by Starkey himself. Henry Starkey was no Donald Trump.

Arcadia it became, named for the city in ancient Greece that implied a contented, simple lifestyle. In the late 1880s, as timber fell and the sawmill sang, all was not utopia for the Starkey operation. With multitudes of lumber cut, Starkey was continually vexed by a lack of available vessels to ship the stockpiled lumber. Ever industrious, he set out to conquer the problem plaguing his business. Selecting the choicest cuts of oak like a meat cutter would the roast for Sunday dinner, Starkey had his wood shipped to Milwaukee, where he would have his own steamer built.

In the spring of 1888, John Fitzgerald completed the finishing touches on the steamer in Milwaukee, and the boat was delivered to Starkey. Felicitously, she was named *Arcadia.* At only 119 feet in length, the *Arcadia* was of modest size, even for a steam barge. With a beam of twenty-six feet and a draft of slightly over nine, she grossed 230 tons, and was capable of hauling just under three hundred thousand board feet of lumber. Unimposing in stature, the ship was perfect for Starkey's operation and was immediately successful.

For a decade the *Arcadia* served Starkey graciously, calling on most Lake Michigan ports at one time or another. Her appealing looks were hardly diminished as ice gnawed at her doughty oaken hull and scrapes with docks and, on one occasion, a Milwaukee bridge, further lacerated her lower bow. Battle scars were all these were, for the staunch *Arcadia.*

In 1898 Starkey died, and his beloved little steamer passed into the hands of his son, Charles. Charles Starkey continued to operate the vessel much as his father did, bringing the *Arcadia* into the twentieth century the same way it left the nineteenth, shuttling lumber cargoes to various ports. After eight years of managing the exploits of the *Arcadia,* Charles Starkey grew weary. Cargoes were becoming more difficult to obtain and greater distances required to secure them. It was painfully apparent the halcyon days of the lumbering era on the Great Lakes had drawn to a close. At the end of the 1906 shipping season, Charles Starkey put the *Arcadia* on the market.

Where Charles Starkey failed to see many more profitable outings for the small steamer, a man from Cleveland could see otherwise. Like his father, he too concluded that the fading glow of lumber hookers was setting like a tired sun over Lake Michigan. According to the pedantic Lake Michigan historian Arthur C. Frederickson, the prospective buyer of the *Arcadia* had designs on using the boat, with necessary modifications, as a tug to work the St. Clair and Detroit Rivers.

May was a licensed captain, to be sure, but his papers and credo were attained in the mastery of sailing ships. May never had charge of a steamship. Through his long tenure on the lakes, his association with sailors provided him with contacts and possible appointments to crew the *Arcadia.* The first to sign on with his business proposition was a fellow Clevelander, Captain Carlton Graves. Graves joining forces with May added the needed experience for a master of a steamship.

Charles Starkey and May came to terms in late March, and on the twenty-seventh, May took possession of the *Arcadia.* The exact purchase price is unknown, but May did insure the steamer for the nominal sum of $4,000. With Graves and the addition of engineer Fred Pringle, the fit-out process began.

When the *Arcadia* was poised to lap the cold waters of Lake Michigan once more, May was concerned about a major obstacle to overcome before he could sail his recent purchase over the tip of the mitten of Michigan and down Lake Huron. It was the adversarial element ice, and at the Straits of Mackinac it was abundant.

The lakes themselves were comparatively ice-free with the exceptions of a few arctic trouble spots. No surprise that above the Soo, ice was thick and impenetrable on Whitefish Bay. On Lake Erie, off Point Pelee, a large floe of ice posed a menace to up- and downbound navigation. Green Bay was ice-choked, and there were the Straits where ice would windrow, then reorganize elsewhere in packs as the wind pushed it, making conditions troublesome.

Despite the hopscotching ice in the Straits driven by tug-of-war winds, the navigation season on Lake Michigan began early and auspiciously. On March 21, the steamer *Marion* sailed from Chicago to Ludington with a load of salt. Her crew reported encountering practically no ice in the trip up the lake. Spurred by the promising news, other steamers and passenger and freight operators commenced the early season runs.

For May and the *Arcadia*, the marauding ice in the Straits, in contrast to the open waters of Lake Michigan, presented an opportunity for May to pocket a few bucks before initiating his new steamboat in her new life as a tug. That opportunity knocked on a familiar hardwood door. The *Arcadia* could pick up a few lumber cargoes for cross-lake deliveries, a propitious opportunity for May; the *Arcadia* could work while waiting for the ice at the Straits to dissipate.

On April 2, as May and contingent prepped the boat for a familiar lumber run, one improvement to the *Arcadia* was the installation of a new steam steering gear. Four days later, May brought her out of her home port and into Manistee, where she would take on a deck load of hardwood at the State Lumber Company. When the 180,000 board feet of lumber were aboard, the *Arcadia* nosed out of Manistee and set course for Two Rivers, Wisconsin, almost directly across the lake. After delivery to the Hamilton Manufacturing Company, *Arcadia* returned to Manistee. May's first trip as a steamboat captain was consummated.

For two young men who worked the ship on the trip, Nels Schubert and Carl Hanson, the episode was dubious. It might have been comical if ramifications hadn't been so great. Hanson, a Manistee man and fireman on the *Arcadia*, gave his account of the trip: with Graves the only experienced steam navigator, the ship left Manistee late due to engine-room repairs. Making slow progress to Two Rivers, they had difficulty picking up the harbor lights through falling snow, so the boat hove to and waited for daybreak. Hanson claimed that during the trip, water entered through the ash chute and he worked in the fire hold in water almost up to his knees. Returning to Manistee, the overworked Pringle would fall asleep, being awakened by the fireman to answer signals from the bridge. Arriving off Manistee that night, May held the *Arcadia* until morning. The new steering gear had gremlins, and a crowd watched her as she steered drunkenly down the river and bumped through the upper bridge. Despite this, to Hanson the *Arcadia* didn't seem unseaworthy, just undermanned.

The spring of 1907 on Lake Michigan would prove that in lieu of the inviting open waters, a hellish situation was brewing. Demonic winds were waiting in ambush, winds that would push the seas of the lake into frightening heights. It would be no ephemeral blow that would quickly spend itself; on the contrary, there would be a protracted wind visiting all compass points. It would fall into temporary lulls, as if to catch its breath, only to howl again. It would strike with heavy velocity in one sector while abating in others.

This began in earnest on April 8, blowing from the northwest. Increasing steadily to gale force, the winds peppered virtually the lower two-thirds of Lake Michigan. All along the western shore of Michigan, vessels stayed in port or quickly ran for shelter. At St. Joseph, two unscheduled visitors rolled into the refuge of the harbor, the steel passenger steamer *Puritan* and the veteran lake boat and passenger carrier *Frontenac.* As night came on, snow developed, driven by winds that stayed above forty miles per hour. At Muskegon, eighty miles north of St. Joseph, steamboats and schooners stayed snug to their docks. The Goodrich Transit Company announced that the scheduled sailing by the *City of Racine* to Chicago was canceled. The miserable conditions persisted throughout the night.

Early the next morning the opulent Graham & Morton Line sidewheel steamer *City of Chicago* eased away from her namesake city into the chop of the big lake. Her course was set for Holland, Michigan, and the staccato choppiness she experienced leaving Chicago escalated into something far more violent. As the steamer began taking an unbroken wave of water against her forest-green hull, the captain of the ship sagaciously altered course. With strong winds pushing the surging water over her stern rail, the *City of Chicago* checked into the port of St. Joseph to join the *Puritan* and the *Frontenac.*

Had one been able to see the harbor scene that day through the billowing snow, it would have been a sight to behold. On April 10, locals from St. Joseph were wondering about the last time steamers were held so long in port by such foul weather. With coal smoke swirling with driven snow, the three passenger boats waited. If colorful were an apt description of St. Joseph harbor, it would apply also to all of the Lake Michigan environs.

Chugging down the lee shore that day, looking more like a frosty apparition than a freighter, the *Yuma* made the harbor at Milwaukee. She was the first boat of the season downbound from the Straits, and a local report described her as "covered with ice from stem to stern." At northern Lake Michigan and in the Straits, battles with ice were taking place. At Little Bay de Noc, the big freighter *William A. Paine* bulled its way through ice and opened the iron ore season at Escanaba.

Another steel-hulled freighter was muscling into the nomadic ice pack at the Straits, the *Brazil,* and on Lake Charlevoix in northern Michigan the wooden steam barge *N. J. Nessen* was heading for the piers to Lake Michigan. Both would experience the danger May felt in the menacing ice.

Having battled the ice in Green Bay days earlier, the *Brazil* was making painfully slow progress in the western Straits when she punctured her bow on an unyielding ice sheet. Although she began taking on water, her pumps and a temporary patch applied by her crew averted disaster. For the *Nessen,* about a mile above Ironton, loaded with lumber from the East Jordan Lumber Company destined for Chicago, ice found a weak spot in her planking. It was opened wide, and in a matter of minutes the *Nessen* was on the bottom of twenty-plus feet of water.

Sailing for the J. O. Nessen Lumber Company of Manistee, Captain Edwardson at the helm, the *Nessen* two weeks earlier had delivered a cargo of lumber to Michigan

City, Indiana. It was the earliest seasonal arrival of a lumber load to reach the port in the city's history. It seems plausible it crossed Captain Edwardson's mind that although it is never fortuitous to see your ship sink, it was a good thing it happened on Lake Charlevoix instead of on the big lake.

On April 12, a day after Lake Michigan had settled a bit, the *Arcadia* was in Manistee loading for a return trip to Two Rivers. Hanson and Schubert had seen enough, though, and they quit the boat. They were replaced by two more Manistee men, John Puls and Harry Powers. Others known to crew the small steamer, besides May, Graves, and Pringle, were May's wife Edith, a friend of the family and apparent second cook Minnie Enauf, Otto Chavalia, and Steve McIntyre. For ship that normally carried a crew of up to fourteen, the game *Arcadia* certainly appeared undermanned.

As it became apparent that May intended to sail, Charles Christianson, whose workers had loaded the boat, mentioned again to May that storm warnings had been hoisted. May was undaunted. Taking the biggest gamble in his life, he rolled the dice of chance and they were about to come up snake eyes. Shortly after the *Arcadia* left Manistee, with her silhouette and smoke smudges dying on the horizon, consequences would be coming due.

As darkness fell, Lake Michigan grew tempestuous. Wicked seas built to harrowing size, and as the wind direction switched northerly, on came heavy snow, pelting everything in its path like icy buckshot. This would be the backdrop for the swan song of the little *Arcadia* and her people: a grotesque ending of shrieking winds and rampaging seas.

On Saturday morning, April 13, Chicagoans woke to the heaviest snowfall of the season. At the same time, with huge relief, Captain Stufflebeam guided the durable passenger- and package freight-hauling *Illinois* into safety at Manistee. The *Illinois* had taken a buffeting the night before. As the ship rolled and pitched violently, freight became entangled with a herd of horses it was carrying, probably to Mackinac Island, a regular port of call for her. With the heavy rocking of the steamer, the horses were panic stricken, destroying much of the freight the *Illinois* carried—a veritable stampede in close quarters on a steamboat. Stufflebeam called the storm they had just battled on the night of the twelfth the worst of the winter season.

In keeping with the chaotic nature of the 1907 express of winds and pause, mayhem and inertness, the storm slackened. As mariners cast a wary eye to the lake, commerce continued with some trepidation. Late the next day, when Captain James

Carr took his steamer *Louis Pahlow* and consort *Delta* out of Chicago, complete with a frosting of lake-effect snow, he was scrupulous in regard to navigation and safety. Carr would lead the *Pahlow* and tow up the lee shore of the lake. Bound for Manistique, Michigan, the 155-foot *Pahlow* was owned by the Edward Hines Lumber Company of Chicago.[1] The Hines company at this time continued to operate boats in the lumber trade, although, as was the case with the impending transition set for the *Arcadia* in moving away from the trade, the fleet's days were numbered. The booming lumber trade on the Great Lakes was closing, and the Hines boats were holdouts.

Though things went smoothly for some time that night, a change was imminent. As the winds picked up velocity, they did something else Carr hadn't anticipated: they switched direction and blew out of the southeast. Under deteriorating weather conditions, the *Pahlow* and *Delta* surged ahead, despite the rough treatment. By morning of the fifteenth, winds were again gale force and the *Pahlow* was taking a beating. An unbroken wave of water was boarding her at the stern, driving her closer and closer to the Wisconsin shore. It must have been maddening for Carr: to have, one, the unexpected wind shift, and two, the ubiquitous snow squall. There they both were, though, and early in the afternoon the *Pahlow* splintered her keel near the dangerous Clay Banks, just south of Sturgeon Bay.

The Sturgeon Bay Lifesaving Station responded quickly and, in a marvelous piece of rescue, removed the entire crew of the *Pahlow* without incident under treacherous conditions. The *Pahlow* filled with water; the shallow-draft *Delta* never felt the bottom.

If ever an element of weather seemed to have a dark, premeditated consciousness, this April wind did. It seemed bent on the destruction of the underpowered wooden vessels plying the lakes, creating a howling lather of waves, rendering the vessels incapable. No sooner had the *Pahlow* been brutalized than the winds shifted again, back to the northwest, and again turned predatory.

Like a famished lion preying on an aged gazelle, the wind churned a fury toward the old schooner *Eliza Day*. Having taken a lumber cargo on Grand Traverse Bay, the *Day* was bound for Sheboygan, Wisconsin, and had begun her trip down the lake. As other boats sought shelter along the lake's eastern shore as far south as Grand Haven, the old *Day* was little more than a lethargic clay pigeon on heaving water. Although the *Day* made Manitou Passage, where the seas were buffered, the

1. The Hines Company is still with us today, now known as Hines Supply.

significant list she developed couldn't be corrected, and just off Pyramid Point, she capsized.

As the exhausted *Day* was about to roll over and rest, her crew of four took to a yawl. Aided by the heavy surf, they safely made the beach at Sleeping Bear Point about the same time when the lifesavers there were setting out to effect their rescue. Though overjoyed at just being alive, the crew of the *Day* would get an unexpected outcome: the schooner didn't sink; like an inverted bar of Ivory soap, it floated.

Across the length and breadth of Lake Michigan were ships and inventions of different eras. While the crewmembers of the *Day* shivered and prayed, heading toward shore in their yawl, other crews were safe and warm aboard leviathan freighters and ore boats rollicking up the lee shore. Heading for the Straits and beyond were the *Henry C. Frick* and *Clarence A. Black*, and the *G. J. Grammar* and *Charles S. Hebard.* These boats would sail the lakes long after small ships like the *Day* were black-and-white memories.

Things were improved by midday on the seventeenth. The *Brazil*, for instance, had been repaired after twenty thousand bushels of wheat had been lightered, to expose the gash in her hull. The Hines Lumber Company had dispatched another company boat, the *Edwin Hines*, to aid the Leatham and Smith tugs to pull the *Pahlow* off the reef at Clay Banks. At DeTour, Michigan, the number of ice-bound steamers heading for the Soo Locks had grown to forty.

But what about May's *Arcadia*? Silence is not golden when you are six days overdue. On April 18, the steamer *John Oades* tied up to a dock at Chicago. Her master, H. N. Boyce, had alarming news that spread quickly throughout the entire Great Lakes region. Off Little Point Sable (near Pentwater, Michigan) the *Oades* had passed through a great mass of wreckage. Boyce said it was on the direct route from Ludington to Chicago, adding, "I was unable to see names on any of the wreckage, but there were a number of cabin doors painted a light yellow. This would indicate the wreckage is from some steamer. The weather for several days has been very bad along the east shore, and navigation has been so dangerous from the east shore that most vessels remained in shelter."

Dispatches from the Ludington area reported the wreckage to be moving shoreward, and curiously, in local circles, no steamer was missing. The *Arcadia* was missing but not missed. How could it be? Why did it take so long for the wreckage to be discovered?

Boyce's description of the despicable weather conditions on the eastern shore of the lake speaks volumes. Another account by Frederickson sheds light as well. Before sailing on the twelfth, May ordered additional laundry from a local cleaners;

it was decided that following the run to Two Rivers, May was taking the boat to Detroit to begin her new career. Likely, too, the robust winds that built the seas that wrecked the *Pahlow* drove the wreckage to mid-lake, which would help explain to some degree why it was dilatory reaching the eastern shore once the winds shifted to the northwest again.

Still, it would be five days later that the fate of the *Arcadia* was announced, confirming that indeed the yellow wreckage and orphaned hardwood were the pitiful remains of the small boat. On April 23, word reached Manistee from Pentwater that the name board had come ashore with a great deal of wreckage and lumber. At Whitehall, her cabin roof with the bell inscribed with her name came ashore on Sylvan Beach. Later, her lone lifeboat would find the beach at Muskegon, in the area known today as Pere Marquette Park. The little 119-foot *Arcadia* had spread her remains over a fifty-mile stretch of beach.

Alerted by local fishermen, a lifesaving surfboat recovered the body of Minnie Enauf on the twenty-fourth, three miles off Ludington. Frozen to a life preserver stenciled with the name *Arcadia*, she was clad in a red dress with a string of pearls about her neck. She didn't have time to lace both of her shoes. Sounding like the later language of supermarket checkout tabloids, the reporter wrote, "The head was thrown back, and the expression on the face was one of agony. Every indication from the position of body and the facial expression was that the crew had some warning of the fate that was upon them."

William McMartin was a friend of May. An engineer by trade, he could be granted a long, pensive silence at the news of the ship's loss, even a prolonged head shake. "The engines [*sic*] must have gone back on them," he proclaimed.

> We feel mighty thankful at our home today that I refused to make the trip. My son was to have gone along too, as a fireman. When I called up my wife over the phone and told her that the Arcadia had gone to the bottom with all on board she heaved a sigh that I could hear downtown. It was awful for the others though. Early in March I met Capt. May here in Detroit and agreed to go to Manistee with him and take my son along to fit out the Arcadia. I was to have been her engineer. The boat was in fine shape in every way, and I think she would have ridden out almost any storm if her engines had been in proper shape. May was a friend of mine and I tried my best to get him to let me do the needed work on the engines. But he couldn't see it that way. I told him I couldn't go out with him. My boy, who had never been a season on the lakes, wanted to stay and make the trip, but I brought him back with me.

The curmudgeonly, determined May, a veteran captain in all respects save the one most important—master of a steamship—may very well have paid for his inexperience in this realm, with faulty machinery. A catastrophic result could be expected, particularly on an unforgiving, treacherous Lake Michigan.

The day the identity of Minnie Enauf was published in the newspaper of May's hometown of Cleveland, April 25, irony was playing out on the east side of Michigan. At the St. Clair plant of the Great Lakes Engineering Works, the young debutante Grace Davock had christened a new freighter named in honor of her father, William B. Davock. A dinner party was held in Detroit that night in honor of the launching. There is no way of knowing, but perhaps in hushed tones those gathered spoke of the *Arcadia* disaster and the recovery of Minnie Enauf's body. In the jubilation of the occasion, no one could possibly have imagined what cruel fate would have in store for the steamer *William B. Davock*. Thirty-three years into the future she would founder with all hands on Lake Michigan, in the same area as the *Arcadia*, and some of her crewmembers would be found in the same location as Minnie Enauf's body.

Hanson was making ice cream then, and on the night of the twenty-fifth, having testified earlier that day at an inquest into the *Arcadia*'s loss, he ended up at the store of his new employer, the W. T. Hatch Company. With him was the heavily saturated life preserver that had supported Minnie Enauf. Reports said it weighed in at over forty pounds.

There was one more young man aboard the *Arcadia*, another fireman from Manistee, Chavalia. If there is a mythic aspect in this saga, the dubious honor goes to him. According to Frederickson, Chavalia's mother had nightmares of the boat sinking, and her son's body would be found with only his feet exposed, where the beach sand had covered him. Later, when Chavalia's funeral notice was printed on April 29, it stated that when his body was found on the beach above Ludington, it was nearly covered by sand. So, you decide: Is this part of Great Lakes mythology, or is it a clairvoyant mother's worst vision come true?

To my knowledge, a nameboard from the *Arcadia* remains in the collection of artifacts held by the Sleeping Bear Dunes National Lakeshore. When it was on display, there was no plaque or written testimonial accompanying it. If this permitted a deeper reading into the lone nameboard, then it can say something also of the time and a great deal about the turbulence of Lake Michigan waters. Nothing can be said, though, of May's decision to sail.

A Longer Look at the Ungainly *Choctaw*

The *Choctaw* was an unusual Cleveland creation, and she and her sister, the *Andaste*, were adaptations of Alexander McDougall's wildly popular whaleback design of the era. In their case, they were referred to as "monitor" or "straightback" vessels, a design described by sailors as "tumble home," for the construction in which the sides of the ships angled inward and afforded a sloping freeboard that was unconventional.

The *Choctaw*'s launch on May 25, 1892, followed that of the *Andaste* by nearly two months. Already, an auspicious air wafted over the *Choctaw* as it rode the Cuyahoga River in Cleveland. On the day of her launch the president of the company that built her, Henry D. Coffinberry of the Cleveland Shipbuilding Company, announced the planned building of a yet larger monitor-type steamer. That hitherto unnamed three hundred–foot giant would become the steamer *Yuma*. Her overall length would eclipse the *Choctaw* and *Andaste* by thirty-four feet, but it would hardly make her a more comely craft.

At 266 feet in length, the *Choctaw* was powered by a triple expansion steam engine with cylinders seventeen by twenty-nine by forty-seven inches with a thirty-six-inch stroke, fed by twin Scotch boilers that generated nine hundred horsepower. With a beam of thirty-eight feet and drawing eighteen feet of water, the ship had a gross rated tonnage of 1,573 and could thump along with 3,000 tons of cargo beneath her seven hatches.

The time and style of the *Choctaw*'s construction are ironic, considering the tribulations Coffinberry's Cleveland Shipbuilding Company was to endure later in 1892. Two of the company's recent proclaimed successes, the big steamers *Western Reserve* and the *W. H. Gilcher*, both less than two years old, both larger and of conventional lake boat design, would founder in lakes Superior and Michigan, respectively, with heavy loss of life and but one survivor. Thus, with no foreshadowing, the incidents soon to befall the Cleveland Shipbuilding Company could not provide any preconceived notion or reasoning for commissioning the *Choctaw*'s radical new design. Rather, the design choice was serendipitous.

When the *Choctaw* went to work in the early summer of 1892, with Captain W. W. Brown at the helm, she did so for the Lake Superior Iron Company, as the *Andaste* would. By virtue of the company's name, it can be surmised what the duties of the boat included: hauling iron ore down from the North Country of Lake Superior to the burgeoning steel mills of the lower lakes' ports. Going back up, the *Choctaw* would frequently gorge herself with coal for consignment somewhere en route to the ore docks.

Although this description painted the *Choctaw* as lacking aesthetically, it bears pointing out that she became an object of study for Howard Freeman Sprague, a prodigy and disciplinarian of lake boat art. Sprague and a noted contemporary, Seth Arca Whipple, were noteworthy for depicting Great Lakes ships on canvas. Still, Sprague likely understood that the ugly cygnet *Choctaw*, even with the flourishes of his brush, could never transform into a graceful swan. Putting the *Choctaw*'s image on canvas ensured the ship would never be forgotten, and the humble tumble home would live on always, if only from the wall of a gallery.

The *Choctaw* was named for a tribe of native people of the American Southeast. When the Choctaw people were dispersed to Oklahoma Indian Territory along with the Cherokee and other Native American tribes, resulting in the Trail of Tears, a heartbreaking, somber chapter of American history was written. For the steamer *Choctaw*, it didn't take long to replicate in small form the hardships and sorrows of her namesake forebearers.

Early in the afternoon on April 19, 1893, the coal-laden, upbound *Choctaw* had just entered Lake St. Clair when she suffered a horrendous boiler explosion. A hellish geyser of steam and hot water enveloped the ship's engine room, clouding it in confusion and danger. Chief engineer Francis B. Smith would later describe the boat's engine-room scene as he recalled those horrible moments during an interview with the *Cleveland Plain Dealer*: "At the aft end of the engine room on the Choctaw were two companionways, one on each side. At least one of the stairways led to the Choctaw's galley and the dining area. The other went apparently to the cabins of Choctaw's lower echelon crewmen, deckhands, oilers and firemen."

Amid the turmoil and hissing roar of steam, Smith and his lone companion in the steaming white hell, oiler J. B. Thompson, scrambled for a companionway. Thompson had already been scalded. Smith was knocked down once, but he and Thompson were able to escape the confines of the engine room. In the cabins directly over the ship's boilers, the escaping jets of steam further disoriented more of the *Choctaw*'s crewmen. Steward Nelson Chambers, according to Smith's report in the *Cleveland Plain Dealer*, rushed mistakenly toward the source of the catastrophe. Confusion overcame deckhand Will Dunn at the same time. He too started down the companionway. Upon realizing his error and reversing his direction, he lost his footing and fell. By the time he was able to collect himself, he too had been severely scalded. Smith escaped with minor injuries. Thompson, Chamber, and Dunn all perished from their burns, either in transport to Detroit's Marine Hospital or shortly after arrival.

Perhaps fittingly, the damaged, powerless *Choctaw* was taken in tow by her bereaved sister *Andaste* to Detroit. James C. Wallace, superintendent of the Cleveland Shipbuilding Company, booked passage to Detroit to oversee repairs. It must have proven an introspective, and certainly dark, trip for Wallace; eleven months earlier, the time surrounding the launch of the quirky lake boat, the *Choctaw* had been the homely darling of the Cleveland Shipbuilding Company. Now she breathed the fire of a demon. This devastating setback suffered by the ship would eventually dim—not in the memory of those who lost loved ones, but in the world of business and performance, the areas that valued the *Choctaw*'s existence. Following repairs, the ship was back to work.

As for any vessel that traversed the Great Lakes for any extended length of time, inclement weather caught up with the boat in the autumn of 1895. She was then under the command of captain John Ward and downbound on Lake Superior with iron ore, on October 19. A snarling northwest wind reached gale-force strength, sending ships looking for shelter from the Apostle Islands to Grand Marais. Tow barges broke away from steamers, deck loads of lumber were washed away from steam barges, and calamity reigned along the south shore of Lake Superior.

When the *Choctaw* failed to lock down at the Soo the night of the nineteenth, little concern was expressed. By the next evening, with no tidings of the boat noted, concern about her absence caused the owners to send telegraph dispatches to cities and villages along Lake Superior's south shore from Sault Ste. Marie to Marquette. Her owners were eager for some word of the steamer's well-being. With the fate of the *Choctaw* still unknown by midday on the twenty-first, she was listed as "missing." Distress turned quickly to relief that same evening. The steamer *Pioneer* locked down at the Soo, and her crew reported seeing the *Choctaw* safe in the shelter of Grand Island. Some eternal resting spot on the lake bottom had not claimed the *Choctaw.* Not yet, anyhow.

At daybreak on May 20, 1896, Captain John W. Duddleson was peering through the wheelhouse windows of the Roby Transportation Company's proud new ore boat *L. C. Waldo.* The ore-laden *Waldo* was downbound on the St. Mary's River, below the Soo Locks. Upbound and light, John Ward had the *Choctaw* angling for the locks as darkness was giving way to light. Duddleson yanked the *Waldo*'s whistle cord to signal his intentions to Ward on the *Choctaw.* He was astonished when the cord broke and fell limp in his hand. In the squinting daylight with communication between the boats severed, the inevitable happened. The *Choctaw* might as well have sported a large red target on her starboard side amidships, because that is where the *Waldo* planted her stem. After the audible sounds of the collision, the tortured sound of grinding steel ceased, and the *Waldo* backed away. Ward immediately headed the *Choctaw* for shore, where she sank in fifteen feet of shoal water.

When Duddleson reported to authorities that the broken whistle cord had led to the collision, the Roby Transportation Company's managing owner and the steamer *Waldo*'s namesake, L. C. Waldo, refuted Duddleson's claim. Presumably, since Mr. Waldo had been hundreds of miles away at Cleveland at the time, it was a denial directed to the issue of liability, which he could certainly see coming.

It is difficult to believe Duddleson would concoct such a flimsy-sounding excuse. That week in his life was further trying. While he was at the Soo in the immediate aftermath of the collision, he received a telegram from California, where his wife was, and her illness had taken a turn for the worse. She passed away as he was making his way west to be at her bedside. Duddleson had been in the employ of the Roby interests since 1889, when he brought out their new steamship *George W. Roby*, just as he had done with the *Waldo*. He had achieved his rank of captain in 1875 with the steamer *Maine*, and in seven years of employment with the Flint and Pere Marquette Railroad Company, he had command of three of their steamers as they emerged, the *F&PM No. 2*, *No. 3*, and *No. 4*. He and the *Waldo* and crew would later be menaced by the Big Storm of 1913. Only sensational seamanship by Duddleson kept the *Waldo* from foundering on Lake Superior. Although they would suffer great hardship, everyone survived, and his character and ability proved unimpeachable.

The *Choctaw*'s owners engaged the services of the wrecker *Favorite* to extract her from the shoal water. Once released and fitted with a temporary patch for the trip to drydock, the duo departed for Cleveland. Globe Iron Works was awarded the contract for repairing the ship, which was delivered by the *Favorite* on June 3. Repairs took two weeks. Twenty new plates, eight frames, and $10,000 turned the trick. The *Waldo* didn't fare much better. She was cleared to sail to Ashtabula to disperse her cargo, then on to a drydock in Cleveland. She too spent two weeks being repaired, including a new stem bar and sixteen new plates.

In 1898 the Lake Superior Iron Company dissolved. The *Choctaw* and *Andaste* were purchased by the Cleveland-Cliffs Iron Company to add to the hearty fleet of Cliffs vessels. Of interest here is a bit of marine lore chronicled by a fine author of Great Lakes stories, Dwight Boyer. In 1899, the *Choctaw* and *Andaste* were painted in the Cleveland-Cliffs fleet colors. The distinctive livery of the Cleveland-Cliffs boats has long produced division among the eyes of the beholders. The boats had black hulls and smokestacks with a large orange "C," but it was the paint that finished the cabins and superstructure of the boats that was remarkable. It was an unusual shade of green—something along the lines of mustard yellow merging with a bilious pea green—that either became an acquired taste or was loathed. Sporting this new look did little to enhance the overall countenance of the *Choctaw*; it was sort of like commissioning Picasso to paint a presidential portrait. Nor did it last long, only one year. It seems that while loading ore, the *Choctaw*'s and *Andaste*'s tumble-home sides collected red streaks and scars from errant ore spilling over the hatch coamings and down their sides, so they were repainted in the traditional reddish-brown ore boat scheme. Thus, seeing the steamer in port or on the connecting waterways of the lakes in Cleveland-Cliffs colors in 1899 would have been a rare moment of looking down the dusty halls of history.

With the year 1900 and the dawn of a new century, the *Choctaw* would secure her place in the historic record of Great Lakes shipping mishaps. A couple of river scrapes and a resounding thud at Gladstone, Michigan, sandwiched in between would assist in this record.

In late June the ship was making her way up the Cuyahoga, not far from open Lake Erie, with a bit too much zest. She forced the passenger steamer *City of Erie* into evasive action because of this, and glancing off a dock the big sidewheeler sideswiped the schooner *Mineral State*. A portion of the schooner's upper works came crashing to deck and one of her deckhands, George Allen, barely escaped the fallout. Both he and officers of the *City of Erie* likely offered gestures and sharp words for the *Choctaw* as she chugged away from the scene.

The *Choctaw* was back in drydock in Cleveland on August 3. This was a familiar appointment for the boat—for the replacement of broken plates and frames. The damage had been rendered when it had collided with the steamer *Alfred Mitchell* at Gladstone a few days earlier. Later, she added the Canal Street bridge at Chicago to her resume of chance encounters. On October 26, she made contact with the bridge, pushing a bascule fifteen inches out of line and twisting girders and supports, completely incapacitating the bridge.

When the 1900 season ended and annual tonnage numbers were reviewed and profit-and-loss statements were mulled over at Cleveland-Cliffs, the *Choctaw*'s ledger probably drew considerable attention. Pencils may have been tapped on desktops and a pensive chin rubbed. Still, the boat would remain an asset of the Cleveland-Cliffs fleet and the ensuing years would bring appreciably less grief. Advances in design and cargo capacity came to dwarf the diminutive steamboat, but a robust economy ensured that she could still work productively.

Upbound on the St. Clair River the afternoon of July 11, 1915, the *Choctaw* was astern the Interlake Steamship Company's ore boat *James H. Reed*. As the vessels loped through the Huron Cut into open Lake Huron, they encountered fog. It grew heavier and reduced visibility as the lake broadened. Pragmatic Captain Nelson Brown of the *Reed* reduced his freighter's speed, while the master of the *Choctaw*, Charles A. Fox, opted otherwise. The *Choctaw* overtook the *Reed*, disappearing into the cottony gray.

Early the next morning, still shrouded in heavy fog and blowing the mandatory whistle blasts required in thick weather conditions, the *Choctaw* was nearing its rendezvous with destiny. In the mysterious ways of life and circumstance on Earth, approaching the *Choctaw* some five miles off Presque Isle was the steamer *Wacondah*. The word, according to John O. Greenwood, is Native American in origin, and subject to various spellings. Essentially, it means "spirit" or "creator," or inexplicable happenings related thereto. As such, a gathering of tribes about to unite on Lake Huron seemed symmetrical.

Both captains were aware that somewhere in the murk, as the whistles grew louder, a potential assailant was closing in. Before the *Wacondah*'s weary captain, Cornelius Dineen, could fret any further, the *Choctaw* materialized like a specter suddenly showing itself in front of his *Wacondah.* With scarcely the length of time to exhale, the *Wacondah* had cut eight feet into the *Choctaw* between holds numbers one and two, mortally wounding her.

The *Wacondah* sheepishly backed away, damaged but intact—most importantly, afloat. Dazed, Captain Fox ordered the *Choctaw* to be abandoned. Her boats were hastily occupied and lowered over the side and rowed away from the sinking ship. The lifeboats were quickly collected and the occupants were brought aboard the *Wacondah.* The *Choctaw*'s entire crew escaped without further incident.

Fox and the numbed crewmen watched as the venerable *Choctaw* listed first to port, settling at the bow. She then righted and began a list to starboard. Then rapidly filling, she rolled completely to starboard, turning turtle, and fully exposing the bottom of her stern. Captain Fox provided the metaphor as the tumble home rotated in her fatal throe: "It sounded as if a million dishes and hundreds of sticks were being broken as the ship rolled over." Twenty minutes after being impaled by the *Wacondah*, the *Choctaw* was on the lake bottom in 250 feet of water.

As the fog burned off later that day, it was Brown's *Reed* that first passed through the considerable field of wreckage left adrift by the sunken *Choctaw.* If Brown flushed with the flicker of righteousness, even momentarily, it would be understood. He could not understand the irony of it all in the endgame that summer afternoon as the *Reed* plodded through the obvious scene of an earlier disaster. Long after Brown's tenure on the *Reed* had passed, in the darkness of early morning, April 27, 1944, in another blanket of impenetrable fog, the *Reed* was cut down and sunk by the freighter *Ashcroft* on Lake Erie, claiming ten lives.

In May 2017, research divers discovered the resting place of the *Choctaw* in about three hundred feet of water within the Thunder Bay National Marine Sanctuary. It has been described as "magnificently preserved." Jeff Gray, sanctuary superintendent, adds in describing the wreck that it appears like "a time capsule, sitting there fully intact," providing indeed, a longer look at the ungainly *Choctaw.*

Mr. Plimsoll Finally Leaves His Mark on the Great Lakes

On February 27, 1902, at the Iroquois Hotel in Buffalo, New York, fifteen agents of Inland Lloyds convened along with Great Lakes ship fleet managers and other shipping interests and insurers. The gathering included heavy hitters from the era: C. W. Elphicke, David Vance, A. B. Drake. Prominent steamboat inspector J. W. Gasden was present. In a room likely fogged with cigar smoke, that first day of meetings was consumed by apportionment pro rata discussions and agreements. Some chatter about the expense of surveys of boats was peppered into the discussions. When the gathering adjourned that day, it was noted by the reporter—either present or briefed on the proceedings—that the following day's business would open with the topic of addressing the need for load lines on lumber-carrying boats working the Great Lakes.

Some in attendance may have remembered the subject of load lines and a proposed bill pushed by a Representative of New York's Twenty-Seventh Congressional District over a dozen years prior. Newton W. Nutting introduced such a bill, which

---

That this is written entirely from an American viewpoint is confined to that realm simply because I could not cross-reference with Canadian laws and newspaper reports. Two great nations share these magnificent waters and their histories. I worked with what I found, and wrote what I discovered.

he helped fashion, before the 50th Congress in March of 1888. It was detailed with nautical terms and lingo—fore-and-aft keelsons and plank-sheer—and it proposed adopting a standard of "not less than three inches to the foot of maximum draft" in addressing the freeboard of a ship. Even if well prepared and nuanced, Nutting's bill failed to gain traction.

What would become clear for the business of Great Lakes shipping, at least in American circles, in that year of 1902 was that the gathering at the Iroquois Hotel wouldn't host the only conversation about the need for load lines on the hulls of lake cargo boats. The drumbeat grew louder by year's end.

Late November of that year saw the disappearance of the Montreal Navigation Company's British-built steel-hulled steamer *Bannockburn* on Lake Superior. The *Sylvanus J. Macy* foundered on Lake Erie with the loss of all hands. So did the schooner *Celtic* on Lake Huron. Although there was no concrete evidence to suggest that any of the boats were overloaded, that would be precisely the point: there was no standard in place to gauge this.

The marine news beat reporter of the *Detroit Free Press* added to the clamor in a column published in the December second edition. He noted that vessels were growing in size, and commensurately drawing more water with that capability and an expanded payload. If draught increased from, say, fourteen to seventeen feet, which the larger vessels were able to float correspondingly, some of the inadequately sized boats were loading deeper than they safely should in efforts to stay competitive. "Many times during the past summer vessel owners along the river have commented upon the dangerous looking condition of tow barges going up or down the river. They have been dragged along by some steamer when the deck was almost awash with the river and it was not an uncommon case to see these tow barges going down with two feet of side out of water," the journalist wrote. He proceeded in the column to evoke the Plimsoll mark in use on ships of Great Britain for just such a purpose, to provide safe loading standards. He noted a similar application for oceangoing steamships of the United States and pointed out that similar measures to bring it to the Great Lakes had been quashed. He also issued stern words about the evident overloading of freighters plying the Great Lakes: "There is but little doubt these boats are overloaded and to sail upon them means that members of the crew take their lives into their hands every time they leave a port. Familiarity breeds contempt and this is the case on the lakes where boats are loaded to a much greater depth than they were originally designed to load."

A year later, the *Port Huron Daily Times* marine news section reported that at

New York, the International Seamen's Union was holding a convention. On the docket was a call for endorsement of a measure described as the Chandler Bill. The bill's aim was to create legislation mandating a load line on ships. On December 4, 1903, the caucus was urging a legislative committee to push the bill. Only the brief mention of the Chandler Bill made ink. It isn't clear whether the bill reached the floor for further discussions, and it appears to have died in New York.

In the background to these upheavals of concern and cries for remediation to the strife of merchant seamen there was one crucial figure taking keen notice. He was the governor of the state of Wisconsin, a commonwealth that had many port cities heavily engaged in the maritime commerce on the Great Lakes. His name was Robert M. La Follette.

Samuel Plimsoll was elected as a member of the English Parliament in 1868. Plimsoll's single resolve was to improve the lot of life of the British seaman. The egalitarian Plimsoll also held that raising the standard for seafaring safety could be applied universally. His aim would be the elimination of what were termed "coffin ships" by the adaptation and strict administration of a load line on the hulls of ships to prevent egregious overloading.

Coffin ships gained their dark moniker under pernicious conditions. Unscrupulous, black-hearted shipowners would often overload, then purposely over-insure, cargoes, sending the ships dangerously overloaded to sea. When vessels sank, their eyes would gleam. There was plenty of money to be made in this fashion, and human life was of little more value than plugs for the wormholes bored into the rotting hulk of these floating death traps. The restive Plimsoll met great opposition. Many Parliament members were closely allied to shipping interests, and his early efforts for marking ships with a load line for safe cargo handling failed.

In 1872, Plimsoll published his incendiary treatise, "Our Seamen," detailing the arduous, dangerous work of British sailors. In the foreword, he wrote in December 1872: "Working men, is it nothing to you that your fellow workmen, fathers of families, men to whom life is as dear as it is to yourselves, men who have committed no fault, should thus shamefully be neglected? . . . Should thus be drowned by the dozens and score to make a few bad men richer?" Plimsoll's powerful words resonated across Great Britain. In 1876 the seafaring nation incorporated mandating load line marks on the hulls of its vessels. This line was, and still is, called the Plimsoll line or mark.

On March 4, 1915, in the third session of the 63rd Congress, an astounding fifty-two acts were passed and signed into law in the United States. One passed that day set the standard size for wooden barrels for fruit, vegetables, and dry commodities. Another, number 302, chapter 153, had a particularly long coiled title, "An Act to promote the welfare of American seamen in the merchant marine of the United States; to abolish imprisonment as a penalty for desertion and to secure the abrogation of treaty provisions in relation thereto; and to promote safety at sea." It became better known as the La Follette Seamen's Act of 1915.

By then, La Follette was a senator from the state of Wisconsin. With a hand on the tiller belonging to consultant Andrew Furuseth, a sailor and activist in lockstep with La Follette, there was help in suggesting additions to the act as it was steered to passage. Furuseth, a Norwegian and American mariner and union organizer, was a strong advocate for sailors' rights. In tandem, La Follette and Furuseth were a formidable duo for social change as it applied to mariners. The La Follette Seamen's Act was broad-reaching and explosive in its content and would revolutionize the way sailing was done and be a boon to those employed at it. Some would refer to it as the sailor's "Magna Carta."

The act is a massive law, twenty-two pages in length. Its bullet points are razor sharp but anvil heavy. Among many things, the act abolished imprisonment for desertion, made major provision for ample lifeboats, and addressed quality and quantity of lifejackets and life buoys. It required muster and drills. It limited working hours to fifty-six per week and no more than nine per day, and recognized the right of sailors to organize. It established the right of crews to draw half pay while in port. It guaranteed minimum standards of cleanliness aboard ship, stating: "All merchant vessels of the United States, the construction of which shall have begun after the passage of this act having more than ten men on deck must have at least one light, clean and properly ventilated washing place." It must be heated, too.

Vessels owners loathed La Follette and his act. For his part, La Follette may have torn a page from Plimsoll's playbook. He once said, "Wealth has never yet sacrificed itself on the altar of patriotism." Yet for all the altruism of the La Follette Seamen's Act, the issue of safe load lines on vessels was never addressed.

In 1920 another U.S. Senator, Wesley Jones from the state of Washington, became eponymous with the enacting of the latest maritime act resolved by congress, the Jones Act. Although it contained tenets to resolve issues not covered in the La Follette Seaman's Act, the underpinnings of the Jones Act outlined cabotage laws and regulations. Cabotage laws (hardly unique to the United States) were designed to protect trade between two points in the same country. In addition, the Jones Act mandated that to comply, ships must be built in the United States and owned by a citizen of the United States. They had to be documented under U.S. law and crewed by seafaring citizens of the United States. And like the La Follette Seaman's Act, the Jones Act made no mention of the necessity of implementing load lines.[1]

Innocuous it may be, but my quest to track down the application and use of load lines on steamboats of the Great Lakes has explicitly consumed the researcher in me. The empty dock I was standing on after the Jones Act sailed off into the horizon left me temporarily inert. But this being 2020, with the remarkable success rates of search engines linking us to ephemera in our cyber world, I googled the very question of the advent of load lines on steamships of the Great Lakes. Lo and behold, up popped a February 20, 1936, article in the *New York Times.* "Plimsoll Mark Put On Great Lakes Ships," the title read, and under it was the subtitle, "More Than 400 Are Getting Load Line Under New Act Of Congress." I am still shaken by the ease of finding this answer that seemed so elusive, then so effortless to find. The article went on to say, "All vessels of the Great Lakes of 150 gross tons or over must be marked, under legislation adopted by the Seventy-fourth Congress. This means virtually all freighters must be measured for tonnage, depth of hold and draught. The load line is a measure for the crew's safety."

As the United States was still clawing its way through the fifth year of the Great Depression and public works projects were putting food on tables of the lucky, and infrastructure was built and improved, somehow, someone or some folks advanced the notion and the need for a load line on American steamships. Amid these surroundings and restoring hopefulness in bleak years of economic illness, the 74th Congress met in its first session on August 27, 1935. So it was that bill number 354 was written in chapters 747 and 748, for public consumption: "An Act to provide for the establishment of load lines for American vessels of the coastwise trade, and for other purposes." The legislation was only four pages long. It ended with this sentence: "The Act may be cited as the 'Coastwise Load Line Act, 1935.'" Expectedly, nowhere in the act does the name or word Plimsoll appear.

By 1935, Plimsoll was long gone. So was La Follette. Jones was, too. Furuseth was still alive, though, and it would be hard to imagine him not applauding the enactment of the measure so long overdue.

1. It should probably come as no surprise that today certain members of Congress feel the Act is antiquated and should be subject to scrapping, like so many vessels it covered for a century.

After Furuseth died in 1938, monuments to his memory were erected in both his native Norway and San Francisco. It is written that the plaque in San Francisco is inscribed with what is called the "Furuseth Credo." "You can put me in jail but you cannot give me narrower quarters than as a seaman I have always had. You cannot give me coarser food than I have always eaten. You cannot make me lonelier than I have always been."

Brotherhood of the Muskegon Breakwater

It was Great Lakes shipbuilder Alexander McDougall's unique whaleback vessel design that influenced British shipbuilder William Doxford's "turret" ships. The name was a bit of a misnomer; there were no turrets incorporated into the vessel design, unlike McDougall's, which used turrets to support the whaleback's cabins. With fairly conventional bows and sterns, the mid-engine and accommodations of the turret ships featured a notable deck with curved sides called a "harbor deck." Viewed in profile, the curved hull of the turret ships appeared to bulge, somewhat like an overinflated tire innertube. In replication of the whaleback idea, the turret ship's rounded hull was built to absorb wave action with a minimum of resistance.

The *Turret Chief*, launched into the tributary waters of the North Sea in 1896 at the Doxford and Sons yard at Sunderland, England, was one of four turrets that would ultimately make their way to the Great Lakes. All incorporated "turret" in their names, and the other three were the *Turret Court*, the *Turret Crown*, and the *Turret Cape*.

By 1900 the *Turret Chief* was edging closer to the lakes, engaged in running coal cargoes from Sydney, Nova Scotia, to Montreal. Two years later, the Canadian Ocean and Inland Navigation Company Ltd brought the four turrets to the lakes for engagement in the Canadian grain trade. The *Turret Chief* was the first to arrive, and the marine correspondent of the *Port Huron Daily Times* filed this report on September 22, 1902:

> There passed Port Huron, bound up for Ft. William, at midnight last, a craft that is entirely novel on the lakes. When the whalebacks came out they were rightly regarded as freaks. The new boat is equally freakish. It is the turret steamer Turret Chief, and it will run the grain trade between Ft. William and Georgian Bay ports. The Turret Chief is part whaleback and part something else. She is 257', 41' beam, 26' deep. A cross section view of her would look like a bottle and her model would be a big source of curiosity in a dime museum.

So much for fanfare.

The *Turret Chief* became a victim of the "Big Storm" of 1913, the darkest and deadliest storm in Great Lakes history. The ship had cleared Midland, Ontario, after divesting herself of her grain cargo, and had made her way back into Lake Superior and the return trip to Fort William when she was overtaken by the horrible storm. The situation became extraordinarily embarrassing to Captain Tom Paddington and first mate Joseph Phillips; at the height of the storm, with visibility obscured by driving snow and outrageously high seas, both men weren't the least reluctant to admit they had no idea where the ship was in the fomented lake.

Early Saturday morning, November 9, scores of miles from where Paddington hoped the *Turret Chief* was, it was driven aground on the Keweenaw Peninsula of Michigan's Upper Peninsula, five miles east of Copper Harbor. It was driven so far aground, in fact, that for her crew to abandon ship, they merely had to pitch a ladder over her side and step ashore onto the rocky coast of the Keweenaw. For three days they lived in a wilderness shelter of boughs they pieced together, awaiting rescue. It was miserable, but at least they had access to the ship's larder and there was plenty to eat.

With an enormous amount of effort and resources, the *Turret Chief* was salvaged in the summer of 1914. Hydraulic jacks were used to prop her up from the rocks that held her in place. When freed, she was towed to Fort William's twin city of Port Arthur, Ontario.[1] She was deposited there and offered for sale "as is." Her future was uncertain. So was the future of the planet as the war to end all wars, World War I, erupted.

---

1. Today the twin cities are known as Thunder Bay.

Late in 1914, the repaired *Turret Chief* was purchased by the London-based Entente Steamship Company Ltd. This would mark her return to ocean service, but not before a stop at Lorain, Ohio. In addition to the repair work done at Port Arthur, her new owners desired to have her boilers replaced, and this work was performed at the yard of the American Shipbuilding Company in Lorain. The ship was also renamed, becoming the *Vickerstown*. When the turret exited the lakes, she sailed for the tropics of Jamaica, where she loaded sugar. The cargo was consigned to a country not in the least tropical—she delivered the cane sugar to Russia.

Records indicate that the *Vickerstown* was never requisitioned for service by the Royal Navy as World War I exploded. She did, however, engage in an unenviable role as a munitions carrier between Great Britain and Archangel, Russia, a forlorn iceberg of a city just below the Arctic Circle.

When World War I at last ground to its grisly halt, the *Vickerstown* continued to sail, and in 1918, her course was away from the devastated European continent. She was renamed for a second time, to something befitting a steamship surviving the horrors of war and leaving the land of carnage behind; her new name was *Jolly Inez*. In 1922 when the *Jolly Inez* became a fleet member of the International Waterways Navigation Company Ltd, she returned to the Great Lakes, this time for good.

After unloading paper at Milwaukee, the *Jolly Inez* was heading for her long-familiar port of Fort William on her old adversary, Lake Superior, on Thursday, November 17, 1927. She ran aground under curious circumstances, or so it was said, on Saddlebag Island, five and a half miles west of DeTour, Michigan, on northern Lake Huron. The *Jolly Inez* gouged her bottom away, flooding her engine room and forward hold and rupturing her ballast tanks. The tug *Manistique* of the Reid Wrecking Company was sent to survey the ship. Upon finding the heavy damage, the *Manistique* returned with the bad news that releasing the vessel would be a massive undertaking. Things were anything but jolly a few days later, when the *Jolly Inez* was abandoned by her owners to insurance underwriters.

The grit and determination exhibited in the illustrious career of the *Jolly Inez* wasn't lost to vesselman T. L. Durocher. He purchased the wrecked steamer where she rested on Saddlebag Island and, employing his own methods and machines, released her. A history of oceans and wars faded away for the vessel when Durocher had finished with her. Durocher stripped much of her superstructure and cut her down to the harbor deck. Her "new" crew quarters were likely remnants from the original cabins. A large double A-frame was installed amidships working two cranes, one fore and one aft, possibly powered by the old boilers replaced at Lorain in 1914. From a once-proud steamship that traveled and worked the Northern Hemisphere with a well-stamped passport and work visa, the *Jolly Inez* became a lowly, reconfigured barge. Durocher intended to use his latest addition in the stone trade out of DeTour, where stone was plentiful and an industrious man such as he could make money at transporting and placing it where needed.

In 1928, for the first time, the vessel entered the American registry as the renamed stone barge *Salvor.* Two years later, and in conjunction with the Love Construction Company of Muskegon, Michigan, Durocher was awarded the contract for replacing the archaic wooden piers at Muskegon, the connection point between Lake Michigan and Muskegon Lake. A new breakwater and a pier of concrete caissons were set for the south arm of the pier, providing a staunch buttress against the prevailing southwest winds, and thus against the seas running in heavy weather from that direction. The north pier was principally stone riprap, built over the foundation of the old wooden wall. Hauling the stone from DeTour and utilizing her cranes to deposit them on the new north break wall made up the *Salvor*'s labor. By mid September 1930 the rebuilding phase was nearly complete. The south breakwater lacked about twenty-eight caissons at the inner end, and the north wall was shy about six thousand tons of stone and a layer of smaller top stone.

Also in mid September came lingering restless winds and seas, which were steady enough to stop work on the project for a ten-day stretch, spanning the fifteenth through the twenty-fifth. After towing another three thousand tons of stone in two barges on September 24, the tug *Butterfield* tied up to the channel wall to Muskegon Lake. Due to the unaccommodating weather, the stone couldn't be placed, and progress toward the November 13 contract date to finish the job was losing much of the headway it had built at the beginning of the month.

On Friday September 26, restless Lake Michigan gave way to fury. Annoying winds and irksome seas became gale force, with thundering waves, torrents of rain, and a dazzling lightening display. Nearing Muskegon harbor, the *Salvor* with her crew of fourteen was being towed by the tug *Richard Fitzgerald*, and both were being ransacked by the huge seas. Rolling and pounding, the *Fitzgerald* and *Salvor* were within three miles of safety, and it began to seem that the horrifying trip might end joyously in the shelter of the Muskegon breakwater.

Sightseers had gathered, not only at Muskegon but everywhere along the eastern shore of Lake Michigan, to observe one of nature's grand spectacles, the freshwater ferociousness of a Great Lakes maelstrom. The waves and spray created a fantastic scene, obscuring even lighthouses at the ends of piers and channel walls. It was on this day that the small steamer *North Shore* and her crew of six would disappear between Milwaukee and St. Joseph, Michigan, with a cargo that included ten thousand baskets of grapes. This was also the day Captain Charles H. Mohr of the freighter *William Nelson* made a dramatic rescue of the crew of the sinking schooner *Our Son*, one of the last sailing ships on the lakes. Captain Mohr later received a Congressional Medal for the extraordinary deed.

The crowd that had assembled at Muskegon gasped when the towline between the *Fitzgerald* and the *Salvor* parted. Instantly, the powerless *Salvor* was driven toward the beach. With no way to reconnect the tow in the mountainous seas, Captain Thomas Houle of the *Fitzgerald* had no choice except to run for the channel to Muskegon Lake.

Wave action occasionally obscured the *Fitzgerald* from view. As she neared the piers, a gargantuan wave laid the tug over on her beam end, shipping water down her funnel, which emitted white steam with the black smoke as the water met with her boiler fire. Lost in the trough, the tug appeared to have foundered. Screams of terror rose from the spectators, and the most pained man there was Durocher. He moved anxiously about, wringing his hands, and hoping for a miracle.

Durocher got one miracle as the *Fitzgerald* righted, and shrieks from the beach turned to cheers. Listing heavily with her stern dragging low in the water, the tug limped through the breakwater. She was no sooner at safe anchorage when her engine died. An unidentified sailor from the tug, with his suitcase in hand, bolted from the tug on dead run, his sailing experience presumably over forever.

The *Salvor* grounded at three in the afternoon. Her steel hull fractured as huge seas toppled over her, sweeping her with tons of merciless seafoam green water. The life raft was readied. The first two to occupy it were sisters, Alice LaPlaunt and Ida Olmstead, and the third was Olmstead's nine-year-old son, Lornie. The raft was hammered against the *Salvor*'s hull by the waves, and in attempts to set it free, crewman Daniel O'Connor's leg was broken.

The life raft was anything but; it broke up soon after shoving off from the doomed *Salvor*, and broken leg notwithstanding, O'Connor swam to the aid of LaPlaunt. They miraculously made it to the beach, and were quickly whisked away to a local hospital. Olmstead made it too; Lornie did not, sharing the sad fate of crewmen Elmer Lytle and Tony Winserowski. Four others from the *Salvor*'s crew also struggled ashore.

Four men remained aboard the barge; three found refuge in the A-frame derrick, the only portion of the *Salvor* left above water. One sailor, Clarence Brunette, fought to reach the derrick but was repeatedly knocked away by the great seas blasting over the submerged deck of the sunken stone barge. Unable to reach the relative safety of the A-frame, Brunette grasped and held on to a cable, which proved a tenuous lifeline. Ultimately his strength waned, and he was washed away from the remains of the *Salvor*'s side.

As night fell, three figures remained clinging to the derrick. In a cosmetic effort, a line was shot out in the direction of the survivors, but if feel pathetically short of the wreck. The ineptness and worrisome inaction by the Muskegon Coast Guard Station, under Captain George Gatfield, heated the kettle of criticism. Why had they failed to launch the station surfboat, some were wondering aloud. The peril was clear for those clinging to life on the derrick of the sunken barge. Gatfield claimed that launching a small boat would bring disaster, and attempting a dangerous rescue wouldn't justify the loss of Coast Guard seamen should the station boat capsize or be lost. To many, this was an unsatisfactory response.

Throughout the hellish night, Harry Smith, a veteran of salt and fresh water, much the same as the wrecked craft he clung to life above, and Lyman Nadeau of Muskegon managed to endure. The third man on the *Salvor*'s derrick, Clinton Lane, died of exposure, waiting for a rescue that didn't come in time for him. Smith's endless words of encouragement and methods of exercise to keep blood circulating saved young Nadeau's life.

As Gatfield at the Muskegon Coast Guard Station waited, Captain William E. Preston of the Grand Haven Station, eleven miles south of Muskegon, was setting into motion another brave rescue. With four surfmen, Preston set out from Grand Haven in a motorized surfboat, and at 4:00 a.m. Saturday they headed north. Exposed to still powerful seas and inundated with cold water, Preston was lashed to the cockpit at the wheel while Charles Plowman tended the engine.

At daybreak, the Coast Guard boat made its way to the remains of the *Salvor* and her last two survivors, still clinging to life on the A-frame. Preston maneuvered his boat to a position to gain the lee, and with lines poised, told Nadeau and Smith to jump. Both were hauled aboard, suffering from exposure, cut and bruised from gripping the derrick, but in good condition considering their awful ordeal.

Nine of the crew of fourteen survived. One of them, Edward Winserowski, whose brother Tony was lost in the foundering, railed against the Muskegon Coast Guard for their idleness. Winserowski claimed the tug *Fitzgerald* had her whistle held open for an hour as the tug and barge neared Muskegon, and clearly the Muskegon Coast Guard was aware of their plight. "They wouldn't take a chance and come out when we blew our whistle," Winserowski claimed. Gatfield stayed the course, objecting to this claim and repeating his opinion that it would have been too dangerous to attempt a rescue in the wild seas.

Amid censure, Gatfield and his charges at Muskegon would be buoyed by a vote of confidence for their lack of effort by rather unexpected voices: Durocher and survivors Nadeau and Smith. Having clung tenuously for fifteen hours to the *Salvor*'s A-frame, Smith could certainly have criticized the Coast Guard's handling of the shipwreck. He didn't, saying instead, "Captain Gatfield and his men don't deserve the criticism they have received. It would have been suicide for them to have tried to come out Friday night as many people who do not know the power of the sea have suggested." All in all, Smith was a thankful man. But if, in the tempestuous darkness of early Saturday morning when Preston departed Grand Haven to rescue him and Nadeau, any thoughts of it being a suicide mission were then persistent, they certainly were not in Preston's mind.

From his bed in Muskegon's Hackley Hospital, O'Connor, the unsung hero of the *Salvor*'s crew, answered questions from the press. Asked whether he imagined the prospect of sailing again, O'Connor answered affirmatively. "You can't keep a sailor away from the water."

For the *Salvor*, the curtain was drawn. The traveled turret ship reached her final port of call. Her career could boast of passages above the Arctic Circle, a role as a tropical tramp steamer that once loaded sugar in Jamaica, a battered survivor of the greatest storm ever on the Great Lakes. It came to an end with a belly full of stone just north of the Muskegon break wall on Lake Michigan.

From the beach at Pere Marquette Park you can walk out on the south breakwater at Muskegon. It takes a dogleg turn to the north where the pier ends at the outer lighthouse. Through the eyes of youth, I can recall the summer of 1966 at this beach: my early memories of the Great Lakes, and specifically, Lake Michigan. It was an era of perch fishing with cane poles from the channel wall. When fog would envelop the lake, you would hear the unforgettable two-tone diaphone foghorn with its plaintive, deep bellow, a memory secure in comfort of bygone but unforgettable sounds.

The year 1966 was also the date of the next breakwater rehabilitation project at Muskegon. As the work was ongoing, many observers may have remembered the *Salvor* tragedy of the previous generation. I remember the smell of the lake from that period, the cries of seagulls on summer days, and the sound of waves lapping the beach. I also recall the metallic thump of a hydraulic or pneumatic pile driver laboring from the deck of some weird-looking cut-down ship, pounding in a caisson with the rhythm of an industrial metronome.

Years later I would learn more about the leftovers of this truncated ship. At the time of the breakwater project it was known as the *J.B. II*, and the description of the capacity of the vessel sounded like it was straight from the desk of Dr. Seuss—it was called a whirly spud barge. Owned by the Bultema Dock and Dredge Company of Muskegon, the initials stood for John Bultema, I believe. Once upon a time it was a steamship, designed exclusively for the sole purpose of sucking sand from the lake bottoms. There was a small handful of sandsuckers working the lakes, mostly lakes Michigan and Erie. Depending on the grade of sand siphoned from lake beds, it was used in a variety of ways, including construction, foundries, fill projects, and so on.

When she was a fully operational steamer employed in the sand trade, for the Kelley Island Lime and Transportation Company, she was known as the *Kelley Island*. Sandsuckers were never designed to be large craft, and the *Kelley Island* reflected this. Roughly 155 feet in overall length, she was thirty-eight in beam and drew eleven feet of water. She was powered by a fore-and-aft compound steam engine (20, 40 by 30) with a single Scotch boiler generating a humble indicated horsepower of 650. The *Kelley Island* was launched at Lorain, Ohio, on June 18, 1914.

Like the *Salvor*, in connection to the Muskegon breakwater rehabilitation jobs, the *Kelley Island* once knew the lake bottom, and loss of life in the process of finding it. The sandsucker's nemesis was Lake Erie. The eventual recovery, fraught with delays and setbacks and arduous challenges, stymied the prolific and championed wrecker on the Great Lakes, Reid Wrecking Company of Sarnia, Ontario, and vexed the very demigod himself, Thomas Reid. All of this took place five years before the *Salvor* disaster.

Kissed by the early light of morning on May 2, 1925, the *Kelley Island* eased from her dock at her home port of Sandusky, Ohio. The boat headed for a familiar spot for sucking sand from the Lake Erie bottom, near Point Pelee, an inverted horn of land jutting into Lake Erie from the Ontario province.

The sandsucker carried a crew of sixteen, with two father-and-son combos, including that of Captain William G. Slackford. His son, William A., was the ship's steward. The other tandem was the Everetts, father Paul, a fireman, and his son Morton, a deckhand. It was Slackford's sixth year as master of the *Kelley Island*, and his tenth with the company. He had previous command of popular steamers on the Cedar Point run, the *R. B. Hayes* and the *A. Wehrle Jr.*; thus, Slackford lacked no sailing experience on Lake Erie.

The weather was fresh and blustery, and a fair breeze from the northwest set off a gingery chop on the lake. At around 8:30 a.m. the vessel arrived at her destination, about two miles south and west of Point Pelee. She dropped anchor and lowered her suction tube over the port side and began taking on her sand cargo.

A few hours later, the *John M. McKerchey*, the *Kelley Island*'s nearly identical sister ship, completed loading and peeked out from behind Point Pelee. The people aboard noted the *Kelley Island* carrying out her normal duties in apparent good order. They sailed on to Sandusky, where the *McKerchey* was to unload her sand cargo.

Both sandsuckers had port-side suction apparatus, a single sixteen-inch pipe passing through an eighteen-inch opening in the bow. Precariously, the hole the pipe passed through was a scant three feet above the boats' loaded water lines. Once the suction pipe was disconnected, a large steel plate was fastened over the opening.

Operationally, as pumps sucked sand from the lake bottom, they sent it and the water mixture into a network of "plumbing" and through screens into cargo holds or hoppers that were open at the top; they had no hatch covers. The water was shunted along a sluice or spillway to exit the ship as it was separated from the sand. Sandsuckers would also employ additional pumps near the end of the hoppers to expel any access water not voided by the spillways. The *Kelley Island* appears to have had two cargo holds. The space between the hull and the hopper was watertight, giving sandsuckers added buoyancy.

At around 2:30 p.m. the vessel's hoppers were full. She could now proceed to the company's dock at Cleveland, where the sand cargo was consigned. Her boom was swung out to retrieve the suction pipe. Once uncoupled by crewmen in the hold, the steel plate would be secured over the opening and the voyage to Cleveland commenced. The operation was carried out by four men: deckhands Curtis Brown and Alvey Martin, chief engineer Frederick Holder, and watchman Andrew Krause.

When the suction pipe was removed, to the alarm of the four in the hold, the *Kelley Island* was inundated by torrents of Lake Erie water. Instantly, the ship began taking on a list. They worked frantically to restore the covering, but the inflow of water continued unchecked and the list increased. Above deck, Slackford, seeing the impending danger, scurried back to the pilothouse and sounded the general alarm. The crew scarcely had time to recognize and acclimate themselves to the incipient ill fortune when the sandsucker rolled over on her port side. In the desperate, terrifying moments following the capsizing, the people from the ship faced a dramatic struggle to reach the overturned hull, now a surreal steel island in the choppy seas.

Deckhands Clarence Bloomstrom and Martin Everett suffered the least. Bloomstrom never even got wet as the boat laid over and died, and Everett quickly clambered aboard when the steamer completed her roll. His father surfaced once, then disappeared. Of the four men in the hold ineffective in securing the cover plate, Brown and Krause were able to kick free of the wreckage. Martin and Holder were never seen again. Slackford, too, surfaced once. Survivors said he shouted, "Oh, my God!" before he sank. They also noticed his head was bleeding; perhaps he had been struck by the boom as the ship went over.

The water of Lake Erie was frigid, and six men fought for their lives. Krause swam to the stern of the overturned ship and accomplished a feat inimitable in the scope of my researching: he grabbed and held on to the motionless propeller. For forty-five minutes, an ungodly long time in such conditions, the swimmers, rapidly exhausting, would become beneficiaries of a quirk of fate. Brown was able to secure a rope as it floated nearby, and gained the aid of Bloomstrom and Krause, who finally gave up his hold on the prop. Together, they were able to pull others in the water to the relative safety of their steel island. Just as the rope was about to be pitched to sailor William Mayer, he slipped beneath the waves.

The seven men now aboard the overturned *Kelley Island* were all that Lake Erie would spare that day. Nine perished, including Slackford's son and Thomas Moran, who apparently never escaped the ship's galley. Also lost were first mate Oley Kriss and watchman Roland Will. Like Martin and Holder, they were never seen.

While the seven men huddled for warmth on the overturned boat, they were passed up by three large steamers and a tug. One of the freighters was so close the survivors reported they could see men walking the deck. Rescue came later in the afternoon when the Canadian fishing tug *Flossie B* chanced upon the scene of the sandsucker's capsizing. The rescued were dropped off at the Point Pelee Lighthouse, where shelter was given and contact was made with the Kelley Island Lime and Transportation Company. The company immediately dispatched the tug *Fitzgerald* to retrieve the survivors—the same *Fitzgerald* that would, five years from then, be towing the *Salvor.* Over the next several days, which would blossom into weeks, the recovery and search for the dead were ongoing. As late as June 18, the Kelley Island Lime and Transportation Company was offering a hundred-dollar reward for the recovery of the last two victims still missing.

Salvage of the *Kelley Island* was imminent. By all standards she was a young ship with many serviceable years ahead, so raising the boat was never out of consideration. On May 18, the Reid Wrecking Company was awarded the contract. It was soon discovered that her superstructure, or what remained of it, was embedded in the Lake Erie floor and her hull was full of water. With that condition, righting the ship would be impossible on the spot. To raise the ship, holes were drilled in the hull and air compartments; air was pumped in, forcing water out. On the twentieth of May, the ship was afloat.

Thomas Reid realized by then what a major undertaking he had accepted. On the fourth of June he announced he would need more time to right the *Kelley Island*, two weeks to twenty days. Nine days later, the big tug and lighter *Manistique* was successful in towing the sandsucker, still upside down, near shore off Leamington, Ontario.

Now that she was in this position, a plan had to be drawn up to effectively right the steamer. To accomplish this, Reid went back to Sarnia and to the resting place of a former wooden boat, the *Maplegulf*, once the *Pawnee*, sunk many years before. The *Maplegulf*—or what remained of it—was raised and towed to the salvage site on Lake Erie. It was positioned about a hundred yards from the overturned *Kelley Island* and sunk again. Engines and winches were placed aboard the *Maplegulf* and a series of two-inch steel cables were run from winches to the *Kelley Island*. Divers ran the cables around the hull of the overturned boat, and once the cables were secure, the engines were started and the winches began to pull on the recalcitrant sandsucker. Twelve times over a period of weeks the effort flopped; machinery failed, cables broke, weather was uncooperative. Once, a four-inch beam the wrecking crew had the pulleys attached to snapped, catapulting the pulleys right through the tired hull of the *Maplegulf*, taking the whole end of a bulkhead with them. The inclement weather on Lake Erie was relentless.

Captain Charles D. Brown of the *Manistique*, in an interview conducted by the Sandusky *Register*, had this to say: "I have sailed Lake Erie for a good many years, but I have never seen such steady winds from the south and west as we had since we started the work." On August 12, another attempt at righting the *Kelley Island* began. Slowly, she responded. By nightfall she was well up on her sides. Work was suspended until the next day and a crew kept watch over her all night, fully expecting her to lurch back over and expose her keel once more. Much to their surprise and delight, thirteen would prove to be the *Kelley Island*'s lucky number. On August 13, on the thirteenth try, she was successfully righted, dealing the superstitious a humbling poke in the ribs.

Pumping was continued once she was righted, and additional work was done to get her seaworthy for the tow back across Lake Erie. On August 27, in tow of the *Manistique*, the *Kelley Island* arrived at Lorain. Her machinery and boiler were in good shape, but her superstructure was gone, so new forward and aft cabins had to be built. Reconstruction of the boat took less than half the time required to right it. On October 17, Captain T. J. Waage was given clearance papers, and the *Kelley Island* departed Lorain to resume her job of sucking sand from the bottoms of the western Lake Erie basin. The boat may have undergone additional work later still, lengthening to 179 feet and having a change of her suction apparatus.

In the late 1970s, I published an article on the *Kelley Island* in *Telescope*, the bimonthly journal of the Great Lakes Maritime Institute of Detroit. I don't retain a copy of the publication, but still have my file on the *Kelley Island*. Inside is the original typed manuscript, yellowed with age. The file also contains letters from several people, now deceased, who aided me in putting the *Kelley Island*'s story together, and their spirits from the past gather around me at the keyboard.

In the summer of 1976, along with my mentor and dear friend Edward N. Middleton, missed and mourned most of anyone ever to enrich my life in the love of the Great Lakes shipping whom I do not share blood with, we boarded the remains of the old *Kelley Island*, *J.B. II*, then the *Ohio*, at the Bultema Dock and Dredge yard on Muskegon Lake. I wrote the following:

> She was then laid up where she still rests today, at Bultema's yard on Muskegon Lake. Pulled up bow-to-bow, separated by a small scow, with the car ferry, *Grand Rapids*. It's a small inlet of the lake with abundance of green algae broken sporadically by chunks of wood and two-by-fours.
>
> There is a make-shift steel grate bridge boarding the *Ohio* at her squared off stern. I boarded her one day in the summer of 1976. Time had denied the boat's authority to gather sand, but not dirt and debris. Her deck was choked with corroded cans and bits of oiled hawser. Just aft her remaining forward cabin, two saplings were growing, with intentions of growing even higher, or as much as the deck of a former sandsucker would allow.
>
> Up in the bow, I climbed the ladder to her forecastle deck and glanced down her stem. Her name *Ohio* was faded and sore. Her green paint was cracked and buckled, like a parched riverbed, exposing her rusted steel hull. I brushed aside cobwebs and checked into her remaining cabin, which apparently served as her master's quarters.

Despite the turmoil there, it showed signs of once being a finely-appointed cabin. The oak paneling still appeared in good shape, and I recall there being a broken desk and likewise the same of bedsprings.

When I think of *Ohio*, I think in terms of her as *Kelley Island*, a steel monolith that should be given to me if I had a backyard big enough. I feel like she is mine. When I was walking her decks on that brackish little inlet of Muskegon Lake, however, all I could think of was nine men in 1925.

Altruism and romanticism be damned in the endgame. My beloved *Ohio* was eventually cut up for scrap where she rested.

The Ghosts of Philo Parsons

By the mid twentieth century, Dana T. Bowen, early Great Lakes marine historian and had turned out all three books of his history triumvirate: *Shipwrecks of the Lakes*, *Lore of the Lakes*, and *Memories of the Lakes*. His writing style was starchy: rigid as peanut brittle. His stiff-legged sentences may have lacked glistening prose, but his books would resonate with the test of time. Most lovers of Great Lakes maritime history have at one point in their life read Bowen's works. Most probably still have them housed on a bookshelf somewhere in their dwelling.

It was in his *Memories of the Lakes* that I would read about the *Philo Parsons* so many years ago. For an unknown reason, something takes up residence in our memory and reposes in silence until it wakes and stirs and reminds us it still breathes and where it lives. Such would be the case of the *Philo Parsons*, buried like a truffle and hidden in my mind for decades.

Around the same time the *Philo Parsons* unpacked and bedded down in my brain, I had become a fledgling, curious tombstone tourist. Although I don't remember exactly when, or for that matter, where, it began, I do remember the book that illuminated my interest, a recent publication called *Here Lies America: A*

Collection of Notable Graves by Nancy Ellis and Parker Hayden. Although the seed was planted, it would take years before I began visiting cemeteries where famous people are interred.

Elmwood Cemetery in Detroit is a particularly captivating, rolling landscape of hallowed grounds for people like me, not merely for the many Detroit and Michigan luminaries at rest here, buried and entombed: Lewis Cass, Henry B. Joy, Douglass Houghton, Hiram Walker, Bernhard Stroh, Coleman A. Young. The grounds of Elmwood Cemetery contain the torpid, somber flow of Parent Creek. On July 31, 1763, British troops under the command of James Dalyell were ambushed by their intended prey, Chief Pontiac and his gathered resistance, during "Pontiac's Rebellion." That unexpected attack led by Pontiac left twenty dead, including Dalyell, and the water of Parent Creek was said to have run red with blood, giving the battle and creek their doleful name, Bloody Run, as the Native American warriors cut down Dalyell and his troops in arcade video fashion. Elmwood was a field of death long before its gates opened as the graveyard it was destined to be.

During my pilgrimage through Elmwood I came across the resting spot of Philo Parsons. He wasn't the subject of my search. Frankly, inane as it may sound, I didn't even know Philo Parsons was a real person. At the time, my girlfriend and I were looking for the tomb of a more celebrated Detroiter, former mayor Coleman A. Young. Discovering Parsons's grave marker set off a charge within me—I blurted his name out loud, stunned by the revelation Parsons not only once walked the earth but was connected for all eternity to Detroit.

This ship *Parsons*, which I can only bid that I am summoned to relate, via the man Philo Parsons as he whiles away eternity in Elmwood, was the only U.S. vessel of or on the Great Lakes pirated during the Civil War by Confederate forces.

Philo Parsons the man, reaching adulthood in Detroit, was early on a grocery merchant and private banker, with a bank he formed that would become First National Bank, and in 1862, he himself would travel to Washington, DC, to obtain the bank's charter. He served as alderman for the then Sixth Ward of Detroit, and in the early 1870s assisted in pursuing a measure to purchase Belle Isle, over the veto of Mayor Hugh Moffat. He did nearly all the soliciting of funding to bring the state fair to Detroit. Philo Parsons was a renaissance man.

His namesake steamer, built in Algonac, Michigan, in 1861, the year before Philo Parsons acquired his bank charter, was a diminutive ship. One hundred thirty-six feet in overall length, twenty in beam, and drawing in the range of twelve feet, she was a walking-beam sidewheeler, netting around 212 tons. She worked the Detroit to Sandusky, Ohio, run, with intermittent stops in between, in the passenger and package freight trade. When the *Parsons* departed the Trowbridge, Chip & Rowe dock on the Detroit River unassumingly on the morning of September 19, 1864, that began the multifarious machinations that would unveil and unwind an ill-fated plot of misfiring kinetics that would result in a grand fiasco. There was a brazen scheme destined for failure, employing covert and undercover Confederate officers, the nation of Canada, unexpected movement of another steamboat, foiled plans, a thin ruse, and ultimately, a date with the executioner for one of the pirates.

In a deposition rendered later, the *Parsons*'s clerk, Walter O. Ashley, described being approached by a young man the evening before the event was set in motion, with a request that the steamer make additional stops on the Canadian shore at Sandwich and Malden (now Amherstburg, Ontario). That man accosting Ashley and seeking the quick dock hops in Canada would prove to be John Yates Beall, a coconspirator in the piracy plot of the *Parsons*. For his part, Beall boarded the steamer in Detroit that morning. Ashley went on to say, "On my arrival at Maiden [*sic*] about twenty men came onboard. I took them to be skedaddlers returning home, and did not think strange of it, as it is a very common occurrence. Their baggage consisted of one very old pack trunk, which was tied up with ropes."

In the city of Sandusky, Ohio, a second coconspirator had embedded himself in the community. In the guise of a representative of a Pennsylvania oil company, Charles H. Cole had curried friendly relations both ashore and with crewmen aboard the only gunship plying the waters of the Great Lakes during the Civil War, the U.S. warship *Michigan*. The doughty dreadnaught spent the Civil War years on the lower Great Lakes. For the most part, the *Michigan* could be found on Sandusky Bay, within sight of the fortified installation on Johnson's Island that housed a Confederate prisoner-of-war camp.

Surreptitiously, as the *Parsons* was steering toward her destination of Sandusky, with one more port of call at Kelley Island, Cole would be feting the crew of the *Michigan* with a repast and champagne. Cole's notion was to drug the champagne, narcotically waylaying the crew, then to overpower them and seize control of the gunboat. When the crew of the *Michigan* was anesthetized, Cole would signal to Beall in the hijacked *Parsons*. Beall's pirates would then steer the commandeered warship to Johnson's Island, where they would free the prison population incarcerated there, most of whom were Confederate officers. One must admit it would prove to be a faulty plan.

Complete unraveling of the Confederate coup began nearly as soon as Beall and his pirates swung into action, as the *Parsons* was nearing Sandusky Bay. The rope-bound vintage trunk was opened and the weapons of freshwater foul play were there for brandishing: pistols, knives, and hatchets. Hatchets were fundamental to any successful piracy, and one of Beall's buccaneers hacked away at some of the *Parsons*'s salon doors. A portion of the *Parsons*'s freight consignment was pig iron bars destined for Sandusky and later arms manufacture. In an effort to defray such metamorphosis into weapons of war that would later be used against them, the pirates began heaving the iron pigs overboard.

Given the evidently blossoming mission of the Confederate cabal to this point, Beall ordered the *Parsons* to be sailed into Sandusky Bay, likely for reconnoitering, or at least locating the gunboat. Just as quickly, he had the *Parsons*'s course altered, and the sidewheeler was turned away from the bay, churning instead for Middle Bass Island. The quest at Middle Bass Island was to replenish the boiler fuel—wood—for the *Parsons.* Someone must have finally checked the gas gauge.

As the *Parsons* was taking on wood to keep her boilers hot—and doubtlessly rendering Beall apoplectic—a steamboat similar in size and make sidled up next to the *Parsons* and lashed fast to her. Instinctively, the crew of the vessel, the *Island Queen*, began passing freight to the *Parsons*, shouting conversation amid the din of dockside operations. Business as usual, unknown though it was to Beall.

Beall's day had taken a turn for the worse by any measure. He ordered his band of pirates to board the *Island Queen*, and soon thereafter chaos and confusion ensued. A few shots were fired. The engineer of the *Island Queen*, Henry Haines, was reluctant to give up his post, shouting defiance. Then a bullet grazed his cheek and he recanted, leaving his engine-room post.

The unanticipated turn of events forced Beall to some ad hoc decisions. First, all of the *Island Queen*'s crew and passengers—roughly one hundred people—were hustled aboard the *Parsons*. Beall came quickly to the conclusion that this idea was untenable, and forced the passengers off of the boat and back onto the island. Witnesses claim that Beall demanded on threat of reprisal that they keep the incident secret for twenty-four hours, risible instructions that seemed just as likely to succeed as Beall's and Cole's overall mission then appeared.

Rafted to the *Island Queen*, the *Parsons* strained laboriously from the dock, and Beall forced the captain of the *Island Queen*, G. W. Orr, to take the helm. Their progress was arduous—slow like social change, a piggyback ride in beach sand—so Beall ordered that the *Island Queen* be cut free. The ship was scuttled and sank in a very fortuitous location on Lake Erie—fortuitous for the *Island Queen* and her owners, anyhow, reportedly on Chickanolee Reef.[1]

Cole's day wasn't going much better. Suspicions were raised about the faux oilman and his gadfly dispensations, and the relentless encouragement to drink from the bottomless bottles of champagne. The nervous merriment was taking a toll. Cole's end of the bargain to have a besotted and helpless crew consigned to the *Michigan* unspooled like a roll of toilet paper. By nightfall, Cole had been outed as the charlatan he was and arrested, clapped into irons.

As night settled, so it settled too in Beall's mind that the entire operation had gone awry. Whatever form of signal from the *Michigan* Cole was to have initiated to the sluggish *Parsons* to indicate that the warship was in Confederate hands hadn't materialized. Beall had the *Parsons*'s boiler stoked with the hardwood taken on at Middle Bass Island, nudging the needle of her gauge to "burst." The run for sanctuary in Canada had begun. Dana T. Bowen wrote that the passengers left behind, marooned in this episode as it were, on Middle Bass Island, reported seeing the *Parsons* making that run for independent neutrality, pitching burning embers, golden and orange, into the night sky from her lone blistering smokestack.

When the *Parsons* nosed into the Detroit River her speed was checked down. Beall barked out his command for the steamer to be stopped twice in the lower stretch of the river. First was near Malden, where most of the pirates hopped ship and fled into the Canadian hinterlands. A bit further up river, at Fighting Island, Captain Orr and his crew from the *Island Queen* were landed and released.

Not long after Fighting Island faded in the sidewheeler's wake, Beall and the remaining raiders cast free from the *Parsons* in a yawl, leaving her adrift in the Detroit River, not far from her dock and where the whole dismal act commenced. According to the *New York Times*, they, along with a few reported "Copperheads"—Democrats and opponents of the Civil War hoping for resolution with the Confederacy—dispersed eastward into Canada.

To the hollow-eyed captives from the South, incarcerated on Johnson's Island, the fragile and foiled mission to rescue them was most likely unknown. Prisoner-of-war camps established during the Civil War—tended by Americans, administered by Americans, populated by Americans—can still inflict an uncomfortable rash. Johnson's Island was certainly no Camp Douglas, a ghastly charnel house

1. Much of the *Island Queen* remained above water. She would later be refloated and returned to service.

near Chicago. All camps would pale in comparison to Georgia's Andersonville. But death was ever present on Johnson's Island. Imaging and excavations around the Confederate cemetery have shown that the 239 marked graves aren't the only soil locations holding bones in the near vicinity.

Students and historians of Johnson's Island point to the low mortality rate and relatively humane conditions at the camp, linking it to the presumed education of the officers detained there, allowing for a more innocuous setting. Perhaps because learned men were serving time on the island, there were diaries that survived, and voices from those tortured wraiths are here for us to read today.

One of the last men to leave Johnson's Island was Lt. Colonel John W. Inzer of the 58th Alabama Regiment, who had been captured during the Battle of Missionary Ridge. Excerpts from his diary provide an intimate and person glimpse into life at the camp. Indeed, in the first entry shared here, two months before the *Parsons* fiasco, he would mention the redoubtable *Michigan*:

> July 17, 1864—Gun boat Michigan in the bay for several days past.
>
> Sunday, July 24, 1864—The yankees here guarding us have been keeping a regular fire on us a large portion of the time since we came here. For the last two weeks the fire has been awful. Last night, two officers in Block D, Dillard of Virginia and Ingram, were seriously wounded. Such shameful coward the yankees are.
>
> December 24, 1864—Cloudy morning. Clear evening. Not so cold as yesterday. Lake is still frozen over. I would like to be with my parents this evening. Smallpox in hospital. Capt. Markham went to hospital this morning. Not much news today.
>
> December 25, 1864—Sun shined early in the morning, cloudy the balance of the day. Some rain late in the evening. Two bites of beef, bread, tea, no sugar for breakfast. Hog and hominy for dinner. Rather warm tonight. Wrote to Mrs. C.J. Viley.
>
> December 26, 1864—Colonel Hill issued an order today, Prohibiting the New York News, the Cincinnati Enquirer and Chicago Times, from being circulated in the prison. Close, cloudy warm day. No news. Smallpox spreading in prison.

Inzer would live sixty-three years longer than Beall would. Newspapers statewide in Alabama dubbed Inzer the "Grand Old Man" when he died in 1928 at the age of ninety-four. Beall was captured near Niagara Falls in December 1864, on the run and on the lam for three months following the piracy mission implosion. As madcap the plan, as absurd the notion of success, as laughable the plot, Beall was hanged on Governors Island in the harbor of New York on February 24, 1865.

Cole would later be released from imprisonment. The *Parsons* would return to service. The Civil War ended. The circumstance of surviving being the only vessel to be pirated on the Great Lakes by Confederate operatives during the Civil War is enough to consecrate a place in the historical canon of Great Lakes lore. The legacy of the extraordinary little *Parsons* munificently gave us even more.

Docked on the clamorous, densely packed Chicago River—somewhere between the mouth at Lake Michigan and the north and south branches—you would have had to search, but you could have found the *Parsons* in early October 1871. It was tethered to that dock on the tenebrous day of October 8, the day that the Great Chicago Fire erupted in a blowtorch inferno that lingers in American history with resonance and recall like few other Gilded Age disasters. You can still smell the smoky air. The ship was consumed by the flames to virtually her water line. The remaining hulk was later removed and towed to another location, possibly the North Branch of the river, and allowed to sink harmlessly out of traffic lanes. That ended the steamboat's robust and colorful short life.

We found Young's tomb that day at Elmwood Cemetery. In a low hollow of the cemetery's rolling landscape, it seems out of place, somewhat isolated, among aged markers and headstones of earlier times. A deep-greenish-black steel rectangle holds Young's remains for the hereafter. I honestly do not think it had anything to with the clandestine consumption of wine, listening to John Lee Hooker songs the day he died, chasing ghosts in a historic Detroit cemetery, that my girlfriend said, pensive and measuring Young's tomb, "It looks like a Sears Craftsman toolbox."

Nearby, on higher ground above Young's tomb is Philo Parsons's final resting spot. One may see it this way: in the afterlife, in the neighborhood of the dead, they are next door neighbors.

The Blue Waters of the Juniata River

You won't find a finer natural harbor on the Great Lakes serving a city and municipality than the gift that the glacial action left behind in providing Muskegon Lake. Easily connected to Lake Michigan via a natural channel, the lake is spacious. More than 4,100 acres, it appears even larger from virtually any viewing angle. It is deep, drawing the gaze of shipping interests. Moreover, due to the embodiment of Muskegon Lake, unlike at so many other ports along the Great Lakes system, port activity is easily gained without navigating first through a river artery. There is a Muskegon River. In fact, its overall length makes it the second longest river in the state. But the umbilical cord that links it to broader water from the interior of the state empties into Muskegon Lake, not bypassing or narrowing on the direct feed to Lake Michigan. It has no effect on shipping, save the untold millions of pine trees floated down the Muskegon River to the sawmills of Muskegon Lake during the latter half of the nineteenth century. Unlike with the Cuyahoga at Cleveland or the Chicago or Menominee or Milwaukee Rivers, it is Muskegon Lake that defines this port city.

Prosperous, ebullient port cities along the Great Lakes have largely evaporated with notable exceptions: Duluth, the southern Lake Michigan steelworks ports of the Indiana Harbor region, Thunder Bay and Hamilton, Ontario. Detroit, maybe.

The halcyon days of most port cities when numerous boats would call on them are over. In its heyday Muskegon Lake would never claim a lofty status as a shipping center even with its fine natural deep-water drawing card, once the lumbering era ended. Few would likely argue that the port was underutilized.

Muskegon Lake was never an iron ore cargo destination. Only later did it receive major coal shipments, most of them for the power plant generating electricity for Consumers Power. There remains an active cement silo. The city, and thus the lake, was once a bustling center for the passenger and package freight business, and many generations of Muskegonites can reflect on boats that called on the port that their parents or grandparents, even great-grandparents recall with affection. So too was it a railroad line. On Muskegon Lake the railroad tracks ending at the foot of McCracken Street once served cross-lake car ferries. Here those rail cars were shuttled aboard the iconic Great Lakes car ferries that ran year-round to Milwaukee. This unique Great Lakes transportation chain is now long gone. As at so many port cities of the lakes, water lapping at its shores and docks is void of most physical remnants of the past.

The car ferries that once docked at the end of McCracken Street have long since abandoned the space and been reduced to recycled steel. One still exists, the noble *City of Milwaukee*, now a floating museum, with berth and breakfast, on Manistee Lake, eighty miles north of Muskegon Lake. Where the *City of Milwaukee* once connected to the Grand Trunk Railroad tracks with the tongue of tracks on the apron to the mainland, there is today a stoic reminder of the past.

This entity is out of place here. For thirty years its niche was a few miles east on Muskegon Lake, the aged Mart Dock. The Mart itself was a market bazaar that hosted steamboats—including most of those in the passenger and freight trade just alluded to—for many decades. Having lost her home at the Mart and been towed away so many years ago, when this vessel was returned to Muskegon Lake after a hiatus of some twenty years following failed floating business ventures first at Chicago and then at Hammond, Indiana, she rode under tow once again to where she now calls home. She is a vintage steamboat that today bears the name *Milwaukee Clipper* on her bow. In her glory days during her second stanza of life, her second wind, those days of docking at the Mart covered thirty years, and the steamer crossed Lake Michigan between Muskegon and Milwaukee laden with passengers on her decks and automobiles in her hold under the name *Milwaukee Clipper.*

The *Milwaukee Clipper*, a sentinel and aquatic icon of Muskegon Lake, is deeply entrenched in the memories and affections of many Muskegon residents. She still looks sleek and speedy half a century after the last time her boilers were fired. Her current lines are eighty years old: an art deco holdover of pre-World War II marine architecture still satisfying to the eye. Artistic lines never fall from grace. But even as her swoopy superstructure recalls a distant era, by the time these transformations of modernity were taking place at Manitowoc, Wisconsin, between 1940 and 1941, the boat was already a veteran craft.

When she was launched on December 17, 1904, at the American Shipbuilding yard at Cleveland, she was christened with the name she would carry until rebuilding at Manitowoc, *Juniata.* Already she had an older sister, the *Tionesta,* launched two years earlier. The honor of christening the steamer went to Edwine Noye, and she was accompanied by her mother on the platform as the ceremony unfolded. There were many dignitaries of the American Shipbuilding Company present, along with their guests, including James C. Wallace and Robert Logan. So too were representatives of the Erie & Western Transit Company, the Great Lakes steamship fleet of the Pennsylvania Railroad, affectionately known as the Anchor Line, the company for which the *Juniata* would sail. James C. Evans, the western manager, was beaming on the platform alongside the eastern manager, Walter Thayer.

There was keen interest in the launching of the *Juniata* in the marine circles of Cleveland: the boat was the first passenger vessel built at that port since the palatial, elegant, unequaled *North West,* railroad magnate James J. Hills's showstopper. The latter dazzled the public and vesselmen alike with her richness in interior appointments and her stunning appearance and enviable speed. The *Juniata* was roughly the size of the *North West*: 361 feet in overall length, forty-five feet in beam, drawing twenty-eight feet of water. Her hull was divided by eight bulkheads into nine watertight compartments. She was double-bottomed with a water ballast capacity of nine hundred tons. Additional scrutiny shows a cargo capacity of 3,500 tons. The number 350 proved charming to the ship: Her coal bunker held 350 tons and her ideal passenger load was that same number. The *Juniata* was powered by a quadruple expansion steam engine (cylinders twenty-two, thirty-one and a half, forty-five, and sixty-five, all with a forty-two-inch stroke) fed by four cylindrical boilers (twelve feet six inches in diameter by eleven feet three inches long) that consumed the coal fuel and provided some 210 pounds of pressure, giving her 2,500 horsepower at one hundred revolutions per minute, all of which could propel her through the water at nearly eighteen miles per hour, to the satisfaction of her owners.

Conspicuous among those assembled on the platform for the christening ceremony was a venerable owl of a marine man, Noye's grandfather. It seems quite likely she had been christened at birth in his honor, with perhaps a feminine flourish. His name was Edwin T. Evans, and not only was he long associated with the Anchor Line steamers that long had called the port of Buffalo home, he was integral to the advancement of the history of shipping on the Great Lakes. On the chilly day in December the *Juniata* was launched, and with the pride he felt witnessing his granddaughter send the latest objet d'art down the ways, he could reflect serenely on forty years of such relished moments.

In the autumn of 1861 Evans contacted with Buffalo shipbuilder David Bell. What made the alliance and project noteworthy was the construction material of the new steamship proposed, a 196-foot, 700-burden ton passenger and package freighter. It would be made of iron, the first of its kind to be built on the Great Lakes. The vessel would be named the *Merchant*, and its subsequent success opened the door to the construction of a flurry of iron-hulled steamships to follow. In the wake of the *Philadelphia*'s entrance to Great Lakes service in 1868, Evans would oversee the commencement of the *Tionesta* and *Juniata*'s precursors and fabled Anchor Line stalwarts *India*, *China*, and *Japan*.

Thus, on the scaffolding holding the dignitaries and assembly of Evans family members, the pioneering giant Evans represented a link nonpareil to the ages through the *Juniata*. Under his gaze of calm resolve, the slick steamer took to the Cuyahoga River, as the concentric circles rippled away to unimaginable destinations. They echoed from the introduction of the first iron-hulled steamboat on the lakes in the nascent stage of the Civil War and reached far into the future of a peacetime endeavor that the splitting of the atom would produce. The lens through which to observe this panorama of historic and technological advancements on the Great Lakes and beyond floats inertly today on Muskegon Lake.

The *Juniata* was far from complete when she was launched. As the calendar turned to 1905 and inclement weather settled in, the effort to finish her was put on the back burner. Built primarily for the passenger trade and with the warm weather for cruising some months away, expediting her entry into service was unnecessary. This was also an era, particularly the year 1905, of spectacular growth in shipping operations on the lakes in the bulk cargo trades. New freighters were being built at a feverish pace, and to extraordinary lengths and sizes. The entry into service in 1904 of the *Augustus B. Wolvin*, a gargantuan with a whopping 560 feet of length, which set the shipping realm of Great Lakes operators on its collective ear, led a charge of several more boats of mid-five-hundred-foot lengths in 1905. Some would enter service before the *Juniata*, even though they were launched weeks and even months after her.

When the *Juniata* arrived at Detroit on her maiden voyage, May 15, 1905, on board was none other than the man credited with her design, the most celebrated marine architect and engineer on the Great Lakes and in the national canon as well, the dean himself, Frank E. Kirby. The *Juniata* nosed up prow-to-prow with her sister *Tionesta* ever so briefly. What a sight to behold. The appealing colors of the Anchor Line boats, white over green hulls and white cabins accented by yellow spars and a scarlet smokestack, were a marvel. As the latter pulled away with salutatory throaty blasts from her whistle, the crowd that had assembled ogled and expressed appreciation. The marine news reporter from the *Detroit Free Press* toured the *Juniata* and absorbed the ship's features and appointments, asking the assembled brass of ownership and shipbuilders how they felt about their latest creation. He was given a glib, deadpan answer: "She'll do."

Kirby asserted his satisfaction with the steamer. The scribe, meanwhile, went about his tour of the *Juniata* and related details of his discoveries and impressions. He noted that the *Juniata* boasted fourteen exclusive parlor rooms, six more than the *Tionesta*. He was impressed—probably like most—at the Mexican mahogany used on the woodwork, including the social room, music room, and dining room. This latter held 170 eating patrons in full capacity. The galley was crowded with no less than ten toiling away at a time, including the likes of a "first class baker and an expert butcher." Among the most modern of kitchen conveniences was a "patent egg cooker." No further details about this clever device were forthcoming, unfortunately.

The dining room was on the promenade deck, and at one end of the room a painting depicted a Native American woman in a canoe, paddling the blue Juniata River. At the other end of the room was a Native American man, her suitor perhaps, awaiting her approach. The *Juniata*, like the *Tionesta*, was named after a river that flows in the state of Pennsylvania. Ascending to the promenade deck level from below to dine on haute cuisine could be achieved via an interior staircase, the bannisters of which featured elegant mahogany scrollwork. Above this and at the entry to the dining room was another painting, of another woman. This was a muse, an allegoric vision, and at her feet a ribbon read, "And sweet the coming on of grateful evening mild."

Overall, the *Juniata* carried a crew of one hundred and ten. She was brought out by Captain Edward Martin, himself transferred over to her from the *Tionesta*.

Martin had worked his way up through the ranks, commencing his employment with the Anchor Line at the tender age of fourteen, in 1879.

Having delighted the gathering at Detroit, the *Juniata* set sail for Chicago, where a similar reception was anticipated, including welcoming aboard members of the Chicago Board of Trade. The fanfare would continue with a following trip to Milwaukee, where, the *Detroit Free Press* reporter added, "A crack Milwaukee band has been engaged."

As the *Tionesta* and *Juniata* began service for the 1905 navigation season, they would run in opposite directions between Buffalo and Duluth. Detroit would be the only intermediate point to dock on the ten-day round-trip voyage.

On Thursday afternoon, June 15, 1905, the *Harriet A. Hart*, a workhorse vessel of the Green Bay Transportation Company, with Captain Joseph Corrigan, was steaming her short route to DeTour, Michigan, from Mackinaw City of the same state, when fire broke out. Perilous for any ship, fire was more so for the *Hart*, which was built of wood. Some three miles from DeTour, the crew and seven passengers exhaled a sigh of relief. Streaking toward their stricken steamer was the shining new *Juniata*. The big Anchor Line vessel pulled alongside the burning *Hart* and took aboard the crew and passengers in a daring and deft bit of rescue. The fire totally consumed the *Hart*, rendering her a charred total loss. Captain Martin of the *Juniata*, ever a humble man, could take pride in a nifty piece of rescue, and those grateful people plucked from the floating inferno would sing his praises for the rest of their days.

Frigid wind whistling over Lake Erie on December 20, 1911, rose in proportion to gale strength. Lashed to docks on the Blackwell Canal of the Buffalo River—later renamed City Ship Canal—a vast winter lay-up fleet pulled at the mooring lines as the banshee winds shrieked through the city. The big bulk freighter *B. F. Berry* slipped her tether and struck the nearby Lehigh Valley steamer *Seneca*, but this resulted in little more than paint swapping. The W. H. Becker-managed Interstate Steamship Company's *James Laughlin* was torn free from her lines, and when blown across the canal, she rumbled into the *Juniata*. The *Juniata* suffered damage to some cabins and bulwarks; three hull plates were crumpled and had to be replaced. Relatively minor, this may have been the first misadventure in the steamer's young career, and one for which she was not culpable.

Far from the Great Lakes, on the North Atlantic Ocean, a calamitous event in April 1912 would have profound effects on the operations of global shipping. The sinking of the *Titanic* on her maiden voyage sent a shock wave around the world.

One glaring shortfall in the famous marine disaster was the appalling lack of lifeboats on the "unsinkable" ship, contributing greatly to the staggering loss of life. The paucity of lifeboats was hastily addressed on other ships immediately following the tragedy, and passenger vessels were quickly equipped with ample outfitting. Another advancement in the name of maritime safety to ships, including some of the Great Lakes fleets, involved the implementation of wireless radio communications. By mid May, one month after the *Titanic* foundered, the *Juniata* and both of her sisters were equipped with wireless. The *Juniata*'s latest family member, the 1910-built *Octorara*, was also eponymous with a river in the state of Pennsylvania.

The tropical, far-flung Panama Canal and the 1912 Panama Canal Act would have direct impact on the operation of the Anchor Line steamers. The line was a subsidiary of the Pennsylvania Railroad, whereas the Duluth terminus was a holding of the Northern Pacific. One of the provisions of the new act was prohibiting railroads from owning steamships. It became law on July 1, 1914, and resulted in the reorganization of the triplets under the umbrella of the Great Lakes Transit Corporation.

Leaping forward over the next two decades, there would be another catastrophe on the North Atlantic that, along with the lingering Great Depression shoreside, would press an even greater imprint on the *Juniata*. On September 8, 1934, the passenger steamer *Morro Castle*, running her regular route from Havana to New York, suffered an outbreak of fire that quickly spread. Although the *Morro Castle* was steel-hulled with steel fire doors and bulkheads, wooden veneer on her appointments and wooden ceilings in her staterooms along with an air gap between bulkheads permitted the accelerated spread of fire. Aided by strong winds, the *Morro Castle* was a blazing, smoking, floating house of horrors, highly expected to prove to be a case of arson.

By the time the helpless, smoldering *Morro Castle* grounded off the beach at Asbury Park, New Jersey, some 137 lives had been lost. In a macabre daily reminder lasting the next six months, the reliquary hulk of the *Morro Castle* remained in place. It was written that one needn't swim out to the charred ghost, as it could be touched by wading out.

Like the call for lifeboats following the *Titanic* disaster, the inferno that broke out on the *Morro Castle* set off another sweeping change in passenger safety. Vessels employing abundant wood in their construction—staterooms, salons, dining rooms, reading rooms—saw their days abruptly numbered. All that beautiful Mexican mahogany embellishing the *Juniata* was now suspect. And outlawed.

Between the Depression and this other maritime disaster at sea that ensnared her in the fallout, the *Juniata*'s future was murky. Add to this the ubiquity of the automobile's rise on the North American landscape. The proliferation of the auto had greatly reduced the numbers of paying passengers on Great Lakes cruises; the love affair with travel shifted from deck chairs to manual transmissions. All of this would lead to the triplets falling from favor and laying idle at their docks at Buffalo for the years that closed out the 1930s.

The *Tionesta* went to Hamilton, Ontario, for scrapping in 1940. As a similar fate hovered over the *Juniata*, the guardian angel of lake boats intercepted the scrapper's torch that same year. The Wisconsin and Michigan Steamship Company, formed by Max McKee, purchased her. Under her own power, she proceeded to Manitowoc, Wisconsin. McKee gambled that as the United States emerged from the Depression, enough enthusiasm and support from the public could validate her return to service in cruising on the Great Lakes. Even if that service was truncated to roughly eighty miles in crossing Lake Michigan. McKee planned to accommodate automobiles in the ship's hold as well, combining the pleasures of cross-lake cruising with the nation's burgeoning love affair with cars.

McKee awarded the contract to rebuild and modernize the *Juniata*—at least her superstructure; she was also converted from coal to oil fire in the transition—to preeminent marine architect George Gillies Sharp. Based in New York City, Sharp had an impressive dossier of ship designs that would manifest themselves and prosper even after the *Juniata* refurbishing. For the project at hand, the reconfiguration of the former Anchor Line steamer was unprecedented on the lakes. She was streamlined from her wheelhouse aft, fixed with a faux smokestack giving her an art deco look that was irresistibly appealing. There were berths and a dining area; snack bar and dance floor; and below the elegant tapered Sharp creation in her modified hold, space for some one hundred-plus cars. When completed and ready for service in 1941, the transformed marvel and venerable steel hull carried a new name: *Milwaukee Clipper*. Her route would cross Lake Michigan between Milwaukee and Muskegon. She would be an instant hit. McKee's gamble paid off.

The year before Sharp accepted the job to remake the *Juniata*, his firm delivered a trio of ships to ocean service, the *Panama*, *Ancon*, and *Cristobal*, the first ships built to meet the U.S. Coast Guard's rules for fireproof construction. The subsequent war years would bring a flourish of Sharp creations that included Victory ships, cruisers, aircraft carriers, and oceangoing tugs. After the war, Sharp was an innovator for early applications of a container ship and the nascent stages of RO-RO (roll-on, roll-off) cargo vessels. He designed handsome passenger and package freighters for the legendary American Presidents Line and Staten Island ferries.

Sharp was responsible for the design of yet another vessel still with us today: a one-off design never replicated and likely never to be. Sharp's company produced the nuclear ship *Savannah*, the world's only passenger and package freighter powered by a nuclear reactor. It was produced to extend the olive branch with President Dwight D. Eisenhower's "Atoms for Peace" initiative. It is elegant and streamlined and in strikingly good shape, moored in Baltimore harbor.

The beauty of the *Savannah* is breathtaking to any ship lover. The artistic qualities, the absence of the unnecessary funnel or smokestack for venting exhaust of conventional steam or diesel engines, make it appear futuristic sixty-plus years after it was commissioned.

The *Milwaukee Clipper* is a floating time piece, an anachronism, quiet and unassuming, riding out time on Muskegon Lake. The *Milwaukee Clipper* hasn't sailed in half a century but Sharp's handiwork still appears mercurial, even moored at the old car ferry dock. There are resilient strands to her DNA. The ferrous, aged riveted hull plates transcend eras and evolving technologies. People who walked her deck and her engine room were related to the first iron-built steamer on the lakes. People walked her decks who gave us atomic gifts. If you are nearby and listen closely, you can hear the *Milwaukee Clipper* tell the story of progress.

Welland Good

For twenty years now I have been a riparian friend of the St. Clair River on the Michigan bank. This connecting vein between Lake Huron and Lake St. Clair is really a major artery of commerce bearing all vessel traffic that navigates between the upper and lower Great Lakes. During the course of my two decades here there is a singular phenomenon recurrent through those years, pertinent to long-time—often lifelong—residents and their companion freighters and tankers they have observed sailing by for all of their lives/ Alarming numbers of locals are utterly uninformed about the Great Lakes and tributaries, ignorant or simply uninterested in how a Norwegian tanker, say, comes into view one day upbound on the river. This is sort of a Flat Earth script, suggesting that maybe the Atlantic Ocean holds the same elevation as the lakes do, and maybe the waters of the St. Lawrence River screen the salty ocean water and maybe that's how the Great Lakes retain their freshwater signature. I don't know what people really think, but suffice it to say, many of them fail to question or wonder about the parameters of the lakes, such that the mere physical reality of these extraordinary bodies of water evokes no queries at all, only marveling.

When I inquire about their knowledge of the Welland Canal, an alarming number of them, many of them sexagenarians like me, are in the dark. They've never heard of it. For people who have grown up alongside Great Lakes shipping and lived with lake boats all their years, this struck me as stupefying, like someone living in Philadelphia who had never heard of the Brooklyn Bridge. To understand the Welland Canal one must incorporate geography and topography and indeed the majesty of the Great Lakes. To understand the Welland Canal is to recognize one of the greatest engineering accomplishments in human history.

When viewing a flat wall chart of the Great Lakes and not a relief map, one may think that all the lakes are at the same level of elevation. Of course, they are not. Due to the geological expression of the Niagara Escarpment, Lake Ontario is about 326 feet lower than Lake Erie. The glacier's masterful work in creating the escarpment likewise gave us Niagara Falls. Just a handful of miles west of the falls is where the Welland Canal was dug. The distance between eastern end of Lake Erie and the western end of Lake Ontario is rather scant, twenty-seven miles.[1] It isn't the distance between the two Great Lakes that the Welland Canal connects that was stupendous, it was conquering the daunting rise in elevation, those 326 feet, that was.

There have been several iterations of the Welland Canal over two centuries. The earliest had more than thirty locks to climb and descend; today's canal has eight. Oh, but what locks seven of them are. At Port Weller, the Lake Ontario feed to the canal, the course runs as straight as possible to Port Colborne, on Lake Erie. Lock 8 is at Port Colborne, and unlike the other seven, which are just above Port Weller and Lake Ontario, Lock 8 is a retaining lock and does no perceptible lifting. Locks 1 through 7 are astounding, and moreover, locks 3 through 7. Locks 4, 5, and 6 are the "Flight Locks," and with 7, they are where the ships "climb the steps." In a distance of little more than two miles, vessels rise and fall some 250 feet. The nonpareil Flight Locks are twinned, allowing for side-by-side simultaneous up- and downbound transits. Each of the lock chambers, capable of handling a 740-foot, 25,000 deadweight tons (DWT) lake boat, floats the boat to the lock sill to climb the next "step" by filling (or, of course, in the case of exiting a lock, draining) each chamber with twenty million gallons, or ninety million liters, of water. In 2018, the Welland Canal floated an extraordinary 41 million tons of various cargoes. Lock 7 has a small section of bleacher seats that face the lock chamber, providing relief for the leg- or foot-weary, or simply a place to sit and admire the rising or falling of a ship in

1. The earliest canal was comprised of forty wooden locks. Later canals built of stone contained twenty-eight locks.

the lock chamber. Across the street is a visitor center that provides information on up- and downbound passages, estimated times of arrival, and ancillary information.

The Lock 3 Viewing Platform and Visitor Center at St. Catharines, Ontario, is by far the most popular spot for gathering a crowd of boat watchers, for good reason. The two-tiered steel structure gives a stunning midship view of a ship in the lock, and more than any other location on the canal, this close proximity to the vessels is a voyeurism opportunity for not only boat watchers, but also the crew and officers of the behemoth ships so near. Some captains take advantage of this, and I will relate a couple of incidents related to this captive audience that commanders become.

It has been written that Toronto is the most ethnically and culturally diverse city on earth. St. Catharines and Lock 3 are very close to Toronto, and it has been my experience that the diversity of the city gleefully spills over to the Lock 3 viewing complex. There is symmetry, to me, that a shipping canal that hosts vessels from across the globe should see a gathering of the globe's people enjoying and marveling at lake boats and ocean freighters from the viewing platform. On any given day, you can share your love of ships with Pennsylvania Dutch people, Mennonites, Hindus, Muslims, Sikhs, French Canadians, Mexicans, and all walks of life in between, be they from Little Rock, Arkansas, or Little Current, Ontario. At Lock 3, you connect with more than love of ships and lakers—you come to feel the rhythms of our world with a keener sense.

With that captivated audience at Lock 3, I have watched (and photographed) the skipper of the *Algoma Hansa* entertain the gathered spectators on the levels of the viewing platform with a companion stuffed bear. The black bear is the logo and stack marking of the Algoma fleet, and this man lugged out an oversized teddy bear to wave at the crowd as the *Algoma Hansa* was rising in the lock chamber. I have been given a return thumbs-up from the captain of the *CSL Welland* after he gave the assembly back-to-back salutes from the boat's horn. It delighted everyone, including, judging by his grin, the captain himself.

Living near the Welland Canal isn't easy. Lift bridges and draw bridges that span the waterway must come up for the big boats to pass under or through, and it chafes some locals—not enough to relocate, assuming they could. In my conversations with locals, many of whom have dismounted their bikes or exited their cars to watch a boat in a lock along with me, the novelty for me will never wear off. There is simply nowhere on earth like the Welland Canal locks. Not 3 through 7, let alone 1 through

7. The Panama Canal locks redden in embarrassment. The Soo Locks blanche. Recently, a friend asked me, when I told him we were heading to Michigan's Upper Peninsula, if we were going to the Soo Locks. I scoffed and told him that once you have been to the Welland, the Soo is like windsurfing on a duck pond.

In the summer of 2016, I pulled up to Lock 5, one of the three twinned Flight Locks, to an unusually large gathering at the spot. It turned out to be a prized catch: the magnificent *Pride of Baltimore* and the replica Viking ship *Draken Harald Harfagre* (Harold the Fair Haired) were locking up. At Lock 7, you could smell the cloying scent of freshly hewn timber from the Fair Haired as it eased by. I engaged in conversation a couple I would learn were from Iowa City, and one of them said to me, "We didn't know this place existed. We came for Niagara Falls and someone suggested we see this. I'm not sure this isn't better" As his voice trailed off, my rejoinder to him was that I understood his sentiment: I had come to the Welland Canal two or three times before I finally made the short trek to Niagara Falls.

My most recent trip to the Welland Canal was in the summer of 2019. At Port Colborne, it was the annual Canal Days festival and celebration. In addition to the gustatory delights available, I purchased a ticket for a cruise on the Canadian turned tall ship, the *Empire Sandy*. It turned into an idyllic serene night on Lake Erie. As I chatted with a man from the city of Welland—on the canal, as you would expect—he began relating some of his memories from youth. There were few barriers to the canal then, and people could get even closer to the ships as they slowly moved up and down. He told me that he and family members and friends would pitch coins or small souvenirs to anxious crewmembers of foreign vessels, and they would flip some memento of their homeland in return. In those times, the name of the port lettered across the stern of a ship would likely reflect the city from which it hailed. Not so much today. A ship from Egypt, for example, will likely be registered to Limassol, Cyprus, and a Polish steamship liner to Nassau, Bahamas.

But still they come, to the delight and enjoyment of anyone who loves boat watching with a clear consciousness, without worries about the invasive threat of quagga mussels or round gobies. One can point to the scenic wonders of our Great Lakes, be it the islands and dunes of northern Lake Michigan or the wild regions of Lake Superior or Georgian Bay. You name your treasured spot, and I will probably respond in applause. For me, the work of the glaciers and the Niagara Escarpment keep me nosed toward Thorold and St. Catharines. See you on the Lock 3 viewing platform someday.

Glossary

abeam: at right angles to the fore-and-aft line

astern: behind or toward the rear of a ship

athwart: from side to side; crosswise

bark or **barque:** a ship with three masts, square-rigged on the first two masts and fore-and-aft rigged on the other

beam: width of a ship

bow: forward part of the hull of a ship or boat

bowsprit: pole or spar projecting forward from the bow of a ship; ropes from this help to steady sails and masts

breeches buoy: a canvas seat in the form of breeches hung from a lifebuoy running on a hawser and used to haul persons from one ship to another or from ship to shore, especially in rescue operations

bridge: main control center of a ship

capstan: any of various windlasses, rotated in a horizontal plane by hand or machinery for winding in ropes, cables, and so on

---

Definitions culled from *Webster's American Dictionary College Edition*, Fourth Edition; the *Thorndike Barnhart Dictionary*; and *Wikipedia*.

centerboard: a pivoted board that can be lowered through the keel of a sailboat (or sailing ship) to reduce sideways movement

draft: distance between the waterline and deepest point of the ship or boat

fore-and-aft: located along or parallel to a line from the stem to the stern

foretopmast: the second section of a ship's foremast

funnel: smokestack

gross tons or tonnage: a ship's total internal volume, expressed in "register tons"

jibboom: a spar that forms an extension of the bowsprit

lifeboat: a ship's boat designed to be readily available to rescue and maintain persons from a sinking vessel

lumber hooker: moniker applied to lumber carrying steamships plying the Great Lakes

Lyle gun: a gun that resembles a small brass cannon and is used to fire a projectile attached to a line of rope in rescue operations at sea; named for inventor David A. Lyle

net tonnage: a dimensionless index calculated from the total molded volume of the ship's cargo space by using a mathematical formula, and subtracting engine room, fuel tanks, and crew quarters from gross tonnage

quadruple expansion steam engine: a compound engine that expands the steam in four stages with four cylinders at four different pressures

spar: a stout, rounded, usually wooden or metal piece (such as mast, boom, gaff, or yard) used to support rigging

square-rigged: having the principal sails set at right angles across the masts

steam barge: a small or moderate-size steamboat constructed of wood and engaged in the lumber and bulk cargo trades on the Great Lakes

steering chain: portion of a ship's steering gear by which the rudder responds to the turning of the ship's wheel; also called tiller chain

stem: at the bow of a vessel, the upright onto which the side timbers or plates are joined

stern: back or aft-most part of a ship or boat

surfboat: oar-driven boat designed to enter the sea from the beach in heavy surf or severe waves; often used in lifesaving missions where the most expedient access to victims is directly from the beach

surfmen: term applied to members of the United States Life-Saving Service

triple expansion steam engine: a compound engine that expands the steam in three stages with three cylinders at three different pressures

windlass: a device for hauling and hoisting; winch
yawl: a ship's small boat

Bibliography

Newspapers published in port cities throughout the Great Lakes region in the period of research this book covers featured news columns devoted to covering Great Lakes shipping. The column headings were varied: Marine News, Marine Notes, Along the Lakes, Port Palaver, and so on. They are invaluable tools to researchers.

Havana, *California*, *City of Green Bay*, Linked in Coincidence

Bowen, Dana. *Shipwrecks of the Lakes.* Thunder Bay, CA: Thunder Bay Press, 1952.

"Gives Up Its Victims," *Chicago Inter-Ocean*, October 6, 1887.

"The Lakes," *Chicago Inter-Ocean*, April 28, 1873.

"Marine Intelligence," *Chicago Inter-Ocean*, July 27, 1872.

"Marine Intelligence," *Chicago Inter-Ocean*, May 22, 1873.

"Marine Intelligence," *Chicago Inter-Ocean*, June 30, 1874.

"Marine Intelligence," *Chicago Inter-Ocean*, June 18, 1877.

"Marine Intelligence," *Chicago Inter-Ocean*, July 17, 1880.

"Marine Intelligence," *Chicago Inter-Ocean*, October 25, 1881.

"Marine Intelligence," *Chicago Inter-Ocean*, October 21, 1887.

Project ShipShape. *Ship Information and Data Record: California.* Great Lakes Historical

Collection, Wisconsin Marine Historical Society, Milwaukee, WI.
United States Life-Saving Service. *Annual Report of the Operations of the United States Life-Saving Service for the Fiscal Year Ending June 30, 1883*, 234–235. Washington, DC: Government Printing Office, 1884.
———. *Annual Report of the Operations of the United States Life-Saving Service for the Fiscal Year Ending June 30, 1884*, 264–265. Washington, DC: Government Printing Office, 1885.
———. *Annual Report of the Operations of the United States Life-Saving Service for the Fiscal Year Ending June 30, 1886*, 80. Washington, DC: Government Printing Office, 1887.
———. *Annual Report of the Operations of the United States Life-Saving Service for the Fiscal Year Ending June 30, 1888*, 20–25. Washington, DC: Government Printing Office, 1889.
———. *Annual Report of the Operations of the United States Life-Saving Service for the Fiscal Year Ending June 30, 1892*, 151. Washington, DC: Government Printing Office, 1893.
Untitled, *Chicago Inter-Ocean*, November 8, 1873.
Untitled, *Chicago Inter-Ocean*, November 30, 1874.
Untitled, *Chicago Inter-Ocean*, July 2, 1875.
Untitled, *Chicago Inter-Ocean*, April 26, 1880.
Untitled, *Chicago Inter-Ocean*, October 4, 1887.
Untitled, *Chicago Inter-Ocean*, October 5, 1887.
Untitled, *Chicago Inter-Ocean*, October 24, 1887.

The Immaculate Disappearance of the *Thomas Hume*

"The Lake Log," *Chicago Inter-Ocean*, November 17, 1879.
"Marine Intelligence," *Chicago Inter-Ocean*, June 25, 1879.
"Marine Intelligence," *Chicago Inter-Ocean*, October 18, 1880.
National Archives. *Marine Casualties on the Great Lakes, 1863–1873* (Microfilm Publication, T729), 1 roll.
Prescott Keyes, Alice. *Romance of Muskegon*, 42–110. Muskegon, MI: Muskegon Heritage Association, 1974.
Project ShipShape. *Ship Information and Data Record: California*. Great Lakes Historical Collection, Wisconsin Marine Historical Society, Milwaukee, WI.
Untitled, *Chicago Inter-Ocean*, July 29, 1876.
Untitled, *Chicago Inter-Ocean*, November 20, 1879.
Untitled, *Chicago Inter-Ocean*, November 25, 1881.
Untitled, *Muskegon Chronicle*, May 28, 1891.
Untitled, *Muskegon Chronicle*, May 29, 1891.
Untitled, *Muskegon Chronicle*, June 2, 1891.

Untitled, *Muskegon Chronicle*, June 9, 1891.

Untitled, *Cleveland Plain Dealer*, June 6, 1891.

Untitled, *Cleveland Plain Dealer*, July 15, 1891.

U.S. Department of Commerce and Labor. *Merchant Vessels of the United States*. Washington, DC: Government Printing Office, 1886.

The Life of the *Hattie A. Estelle*

"All Over the World," *Chicago Inter-Ocean*, October 9, 1879.

"Around the Horn," *Cleveland Plain Dealer*, December 7, 1891.

"The Blow," *Chicago Inter-Ocean*, May 12, 1882.

"Deals and Timber," *Chicago Inter-Ocean*, June 9, 1877.

"Disasters," *Chicago Inter-Ocean*, June 8, 1880.

"General," *Chicago Inter-Ocean*, April 4, 1880.

Mansfield, J. B. *History of the Great Lakes*. Chicago: J. H. Beers & Co., 1899.

"Marine Intelligence," *Chicago Inter-Ocean*, April 19, 1873.

"Marine Intelligence," *Chicago Inter-Ocean*, May 30, 1877.

"Marine Intelligence," *Chicago Inter-Ocean*, June 18, 1877.

"Marine Intelligence," *Chicago Inter-Ocean*, October 8, 1879.

"Marine Matters," *Chicago Inter-Ocean*, October 6, 1886.

"Mate Huginson Drowned," *Chicago Inter-Ocean*, October 2, 1886.

"Movement of Deals at Manistee and Muskegon," *Chicago Inter-Ocean*, October 21, 1876.

"Off and On," *Chicago Inter-Ocean*, May 20, 1882.

Project ShipShape. *Ship Information and Data Record:* Hattie A. Estelle. Great Lakes Historical Collection, Wisconsin Marine Historical Society, Milwaukee, WI.

"Reminiscences of the Lost Schooner *Hattie Estelle*," *Chicago Inter-Ocean*, November 18, 1891.

"The Schooners *M.L. Higgie* and *City of Green Bay*," *Chicago Inter-Ocean*, October 30, 1876.

"Shipbuilding at Manitowoc," *Chicago Inter-Ocean*, August 6, 1872.

"They Will Go," *Chicago Inter-Ocean*, June 8, 1877.

"Three Lives Lost on the Schooner *Hattie Estelle*," *Cleveland Plain Dealer*, November 20, 1891.

United States Life-Saving Service. *Annual Report of the Operations of the United States Life-Saving Service for the Fiscal Year Ending June 30, 1889*, 275. Washington, DC: Government Printing Office, 1890.

———. *Annual Report of the Operations of the United States Life-Saving Service for the Fiscal Year Ending June 30, 1892*, 30–33. Washington, DC: Government Printing Office, 1893.

Untitled, *Chicago Inter-Ocean*, October 2, 1872.

Untitled, *Chicago Inter-Ocean*, September 25, 1879.

Untitled, *Chicago Inter-Ocean*, May 22, 1882.

Untitled, *Chicago Inter-Ocean*, December 1, 1891.

U.S. Department of Commerce and Labor. *Merchant Vessels of the United States*. Washington, DC: Government Printing Office, 1885.

"The Wreck of the *Estelle*," *Chicago Inter-Ocean*, November 23, 1891.

The *W. H. Gilcher* Goes Missing

Bessemer, Henry. *Sir Henry Bessemer, F.R.S.: An Autobiography*. London: Offices of "Engineering," 1905. https://archive.org/details/sirhenrybessemer00bessuoft.

Boyer, Dwight. *Great Stories of the Great Lakes*. Thunder Bay, CA: Thunder Bay Press, 1966.

"Gilcher, William H." *Historical Collection of the Great Lakes*. Bowling Green State University, https://greatlakes.bgsu.edu/item/441295.

McHugh, Edward J. "Investigating the Life and Loss of the *Western Reserve*." *Inland Seas* 57, no. 1 (Spring 2001): 35–39.

United States Life-Saving Service. *Annual Report of the Operations of the United States Life-Saving Service for the Fiscal Year Ending June 30, 1893*, 90. Washington, DC: Government Printing Office, 1894.

Untitled, *Cleveland Plain Dealer*, December 19, 1890.

Untitled, *Cleveland Plain Dealer*, June 4, 1891.

Untitled, *Cleveland Plain Dealer*, October 11, 1891.

Untitled, *Cleveland Plain Dealer*, October 14, 1891.

Untitled, *Cleveland Plain Dealer*, April 2, 1892.

Untitled, *Cleveland Plain Dealer*, April 22, 1892.

Untitled, *Cleveland Plain Dealer*, April 23, 1892.

Untitled, *Cleveland Plain Dealer*, April 28, 1892.

Untitled, *Cleveland Plain Dealer*, September 16, 1892.

Untitled, *Cleveland Plain Dealer*, October 30, 1892.

Untitled, *Cleveland Plain Dealer*, October 31, 1892.

Untitled, *Cleveland Plain Dealer*, November 1, 1892.

Untitled, *Cleveland Plain Dealer*, November 2, 1892.

Untitled, *Cleveland Plain Dealer*, November 3, 1892.

Untitled, *Cleveland Plain Dealer*, November 4, 1892.

Untitled, *Cleveland Plain Dealer*, November 10, 1892.

Untitled, *Cleveland Plain Dealer*, November 18, 1892.

Untitled, *Cleveland Plain Dealer*, November 10, 1896.

A Detestable Day Along the Chicago Lakefront

"Marine," *Chicago Inter-Ocean*, November 8, 1883.

"Marine Intelligence," *Chicago Inter-Ocean*, August 10, 1874.

"Marine Intelligence," *Chicago Inter-Ocean*, September 28, 1874.

"Marine Intelligence," *Chicago Inter-Ocean*, December 1, 1874.

"Marine Intelligence," *Chicago Inter-Ocean*, July 6, 1876.

"Marine Intelligence," *Chicago Inter-Ocean*, September 15, 1876.

"Marine Intelligence," *Chicago Inter-Ocean*, July 10, 1884.

"Marine Intelligence," *Chicago Inter-Ocean*, July 13, 1884.

"Marine Intelligence," *Chicago Inter-Ocean*, June 15, 1886.

"Marine Intelligence," *Chicago Inter-Ocean*, July 15, 1886.

National Archives. *Marine Casualties on the Great Lakes, 1863–1873* (Microfilm Publication, T729), 1 roll.

"Sank in Sight of Land," *Chicago Inter-Ocean*, May 19, 1894.

"Sea Gives Up Its Dead," *Chicago Inter-Ocean*, May 20, 1894.

"Shipping News," *Chicago Inter-Ocean*, August 27, 1881.

United States Life-Saving Service. *Annual Report of the Operations of the United States Life-Saving Service for the Fiscal Year Ending June 30, 1880*, 89–91. Washington, DC: Government Printing Office, 1881.

———. *Annual Report of the Operations of the United States Life-Saving Service for the Fiscal Year Ending June 30, 1882*, 266. Washington, DC: Government Printing Office, 1883.

———. *Annual Report of the Operations of the United States Life-Saving Service for the Fiscal Year Ending June 30, 1894*, 57–67, 278–279. Washington, DC: Government Printing Office, 1895.

United States Treasury Department, Bureau of Navigation. *Merchant Sailing Vessels of the United States*. Washington, DC: Government Printing Office, 1892.

Untitled, *Chicago Inter-Ocean*, May 5, 1880.

Untitled, *Chicago Inter-Ocean*, October 19, 1880.

Untitled, *Chicago Inter-Ocean*, July 28, 1884.

Untitled, *Chicago Inter-Ocean*, October 7, 1886.

Untitled, *Cleveland Plain Dealer*, October 7, 1890.

Untitled, *Cleveland Plain Dealer*, November 21, 1891.

Untitled, *Cleveland Plain Dealer*, May 19, 1894.

Untitled, *Cleveland Plain Dealer*, May 20, 1894.

Untitled, *Cleveland Plain Dealer*, May 23, 1894.

Untitled, *Cleveland Plain Dealer*, May 24, 1894.

The Saga of the *Red, White & Blue*

"Barque *Red, White & Blue* in Trouble," *Cleveland Plain Dealer*, April 16, 1868.

"Barque *Red, White & Blue* in Trouble," *Cleveland Plain Dealer*, April 20, 1868.

"Barque *Red, White & Blue* in Trouble," *Cleveland Plain Dealer*, April 22, 1868.

"Cargo Grain Wet," *Chicago Inter-Ocean*, May 2, 1882.

"Collision on Lake Erie," *Cleveland Plain Dealer*, May 21, 1867.

"Collision Outside," *Cleveland Plain Dealer*, October 18, 1873.

"Fatal Losses . . . Her Consort Pounds to Pieces," *Cleveland Plain Dealer*, October 19, 1895.

Historical Collection of the Great Lakes, Bowling Green State University, on Bailey brothers shipbuilding on Cunningham Creek, https://greatlakes.bgsu.edu.

"Marine Intelligence," *Chicago Inter-Ocean*, November 7, 1878.

"Marine Intelligence," *Chicago Inter-Ocean*, August 6, 1884.

"Marine Notes," *Cleveland Plain Dealer*, November 10, 1886.

"Marine Notes," *Cleveland Plain Dealer*, October 13, 1895.

"Marine Notes," *Cleveland Plain Dealer*, October 18, 1895.

National Archives. *Marine Casualties on the Great Lakes, 1863–1873* (Microfilm Publication, T729), 1 roll.

"Our Detroit Letter," *Cleveland Plain Dealer*, May 7, 1872.

"Our Detroit Letter," *Cleveland Plain Dealer*, May 8, 1872.

"*Red White and Blue*," *Historical Collection of the Great Lakes.* Bowling Green State University, https://greatlakes.bgsu.edu/item/438724.

"The *Red White and Blue* Ashore," *Chicago Inter-Ocean*, August 26, 1881.

"A Terrible Experience," *Cleveland Plain Dealer*, October 18, 1886.

"A Terrible Experience," *Cleveland Plain Dealer*, October 21, 1886.

"A Terrible Experience," *Cleveland Plain Dealer*, October 25, 1886.

"Tidings Over the Wires," *Chicago Inter-Ocean*, November 29, 1879.

"Turning Up," *Chicago Inter-Ocean*, December 9, 1883.

United States Life-Saving Service. *Annual Report of the Operations of the United States Life-Saving Service for the Fiscal Year Ending June 30, 1893*, 226. Washington, DC: Government Printing Office, 1894.

Untitled, *Racine Weekly Advocate*, August 30, 1865.

Untitled, *Racine Weekly Advocate*, June 13, 1866.

Untitled, *Cleveland Plain Dealer*, September 10, 1870.

Untitled, *Cleveland Plain Dealer*, September 23, 1872.

White, Richard. *The Republic for Which It Stands: The United States During Reconstruction and the Gilded Age, 1865–1896.* New York: Oxford University Press, 2019.

The *Eastland* Sets Sail

Boyer, Dwight. *True Tales of the Great Lakes.* Thunder Bay, CA: Thunder Bay Press, 1976.

"Challenge Accepted," *Port Huron Daily Times*, August 8, 1903.

"Hard Luck," *Port Huron Daily Times*, July 25, 1903.

"Is Easy Winner," *Port Huron Daily Times*, July 21, 1903.

"Marine News," *Detroit Free Press*, November 23, 1902.

"Marine Notes," *Port Huron Daily Times*, September 1, 1903.

"May Settle," *Port Huron Daily Times*, August 19, 1903.

"More Breakers," *Port Huron Daily Times*, August 17, 1903.

"Potato Strike Failed," *Port Huron Daily Times*, August 17, 1903.

"Replacement of Pereue Is Announced," *Port Huron Daily Times*, September 22, 1903.

"Steamboat Race," *Port Huron Daily Times*, July 20, 1903.

"The Steamer *Eastland*," *Port Huron Daily Times*, May 6, 1903.

"Steamer *Eastland*," *Port Huron Daily Times*, August 26, 1903.

"Steamer *Eastland*," *Port Huron Daily Times*, August 29, 1903.

Untitled, *Port Huron Daily Times*, July 15, 1903.

Untitled, *Port Huron Daily Times*, July 16, 1903.

The Coming of the Yellow Monster

Greenwood, John O. *Namesakes II.* Grand Rapids, MI: Freshwater Press, 1973.

Marine Historical Society of Detroit. *Ahoy & Farewell.* Detroit: Marine Historical Society of Detroit, 2001.

"Marine Notes," *Port Huron Daily Times*, June 18, 1809.

Untitled, *Cleveland Plain Dealer*, December 1, 1903.

Untitled, *Cleveland Plain Dealer*, December 2, 1903.

Untitled, *Cleveland Plain Dealer*, April 8, 1904.

Untitled, *Cleveland Plain Dealer*, April 9, 1904.

Untitled, *Cleveland Plain Dealer*, April 17, 1904.

Untitled, *Cleveland Plain Dealer*, May 20, 1904.

Untitled, *Cleveland Plain Dealer*, May 25, 1904.

Untitled, *Cleveland Plain Dealer*, June 10, 1904.

Untitled, *Cleveland Plain Dealer*, June 11, 1904.

Untitled, *Cleveland Plain Dealer*, June 19, 1904.

Untitled, *Telescope* 28, no. 5, September/October 1979.

The Reluctant Acceptance of Wireless Use on the Great Lakes

Hilton, George W. *The Great Lakes Car Ferries.* Montevallo, AL: Montevallo Historical Press, 2003.

Smith-Rose, R. Leslie. "Guglielmo Marconi," *Encyclopedia Britannica Online* https://www.britannica.com/biography/Guglielmo-Marconi.

Untitled, *Cleveland Plain Dealer*, October 13, 1894.

Untitled, *Cleveland Plain Dealer*, May 22, 1905.

Untitled, *Cleveland Plain Dealer*, October 5, 1910.

Untitled, *Cleveland Plain Dealer*, July 10, 1912.

Untitled, *Cleveland Plain Dealer*, November 11, 1913.

Untitled, *Cleveland Plain Dealer*, December 14, 1913.

Untitled, *Cleveland Plain Dealer*, December 15, 1913.

Untitled, *Cleveland Plain Dealer*, December 16, 1913.

Untitled, *Cleveland Plain Dealer*, December 17, 1913.

Untitled, *Cleveland Plain Dealer*, December 18, 1913.

Untitled, *Cleveland Plain Dealer*, December 24, 1913.

Untitled, *Detroit Free Press*, July 4, 1920.

Untitled, *Ludington Daily News*, March 19, 1991.

The Remarkable Remnants of the Lost *Sevona*

Bowen, Dana. *Shipwrecks of the Lakes.* Thunder Bay, CA: Thunder Bay Press, 1952.

"*Emily P. Weed.*" *Historical Collection of the Great Lakes.* Bowling Green State University, https://greatlakes.bgsu.edu/item/440626.

"Engineer Washed Overboard," *Detroit Free Press*, September 4, 1905.

Kyleleen Cullen Bartnick, archeological technician, Apostle Islands National Lakeshore, e-mail to January 22, 2020.

"Marine News," *Port Huron Daily Times*, August 5, 1890.

"Marine News," *Port Huron Daily Times*, July 17, 1891.

"Miscellaneous," *Port Huron Daily Times*, September 2, 1890.

"Miscellaneous," *Port Huron Daily Times*, September 7, 1890.

"More Victims of the Lake," *Detroit Free Press*, September 4, 1905.

"*Sevona* a Total Wreck," *Detroit Free Press*, September 4, 1905.

"*Stackhouse* Went on; *Stackhouse* in Gale," *Detroit Free Press*, September 4, 1905.

Untitled, *Detroit Free Press*, September 2, 1905.

Untitled, *Detroit Free Press*, September 3, 1905.

Untitled, *Detroit Free Press*, September 6, 1905.

Untitled, *Detroit Free Press*, September 7, 1905.

Untitled, *Detroit Free Press*, September 9, 1905.

Untitled, *Port Huron Daily Times*, September 30, 1891.

Untitled, *Port Huron Daily Times*, February 10, 1897.

Untitled, *Port Huron Daily Times*, February 14, 1897.

Hard Bark Harry May and the Mournful *Arcadia*

"Body of Girl Is Identified," *Manistee Daily News*, April 25, 1907.

"Captain May and the Burglars," *Chicago Inter-Ocean*, November 12, 1886.

"Fleet at DeTour," *Cleveland Plain Dealer*, April 19, 1907.

"Funeral of Otto Chavalia," *Manistee Daily News*, April 29, 1907.

"Lake Storm Meant Doom for Sturdy 'Arcadia,'" *Grand Rapids Press* (MI), August 2, 1959.

"Live Savers Rescue Crew," *Cleveland Plain Dealer*, April 15, 1907.

Manistee Daily News. *Salt City of the Inland Seas: Historical and Industrial Record of the Great Salt City.* Manistee, MI: West Graf, a division of J. B. Publications, 1973.

"Marine News Notes," *Manistee Daily News*, April 27, 1907.

National Archives, *Certificates of Registration for Merchant Vessels at Great Lakes Ports, 1815–1872, and Related Master Abstracts of Registers, 1815–1910* (Microfilm publication, 3 rolls, M2099).

"Pumped Out Vessel," *Cleveland Plain Dealer*, April 21, 1907.

"Steamer *Arcadia* Foundered with All on Board," *Manistee Daily News*, April 23, 1907.

"Steamer *Davock* Launched," *Cleveland Plain Dealer*, April 26, 1907.

"Ten in Crew of *Arcadia*," *Manistee Daily News*, April 24, 1907.

"Tied Up by Storm," *Cleveland Plain Dealer*, April 10, 1907.

United States Life-Saving Service. *Annual Report of the Operations of the United States Life-Saving Service for the Fiscal Year Ending June 30, 1907*, 248. Washington, DC: Government Printing Office, 1908.

Untitled, *Cleveland Plain Dealer*, October 30, 1892.

Untitled, *Cleveland Plain Dealer*, November 25, 1894.

Untitled, *Cleveland Plain Dealer*, April 9, 1907.

Untitled, *Cleveland Plain Dealer*, April 11, 1907.

Untitled, *Cleveland Plain Dealer*, April 14, 1907.

Untitled, *Cleveland Plain Dealer*, April 18, 1907.

Untitled, *Cleveland Plain Dealer*, April 25, 1907.

Untitled, *Manistee Daily News*, April 29, 1907.

A Longer Look at the Ungainly *Choctaw*

"Along the Lakes," *Cleveland Plain Dealer*, May 26, 1892.

"Boats Collide and All Onboard Lost," *Milwaukee Sentinel*, July 13, 1915.

Boyer, Dwight. *Strange Adventures of the Great Lakes.* Thunder Bay, CA: Thunder Bay Press, 1974.

"Cause of the Explosion," *Cleveland Plain Dealer*, April 26, 1893.

"*Choctaw* in Drydock," *Cleveland Plain Dealer*, June 4, 1896.

"*Choctaw* Not to Blame," *Cleveland Plain Dealer*, May 25, 1896.

"Collision at Gladstone," *Cleveland Plain Dealer*, August 4, 1900.

"Collision in the River," *Cleveland Plain Dealer*, June 29, 1900.

"Disaster," *Cleveland Plain Dealer*, April 20, 1893.

"Entire Crew of *Choctaw* Is Saved from Drowning," *Milwaukee Sentinel*, July 14, 1915.

"Lake Marine News," *Cleveland Plain Dealer*, April 1, 1892.

Mansfield, J. B. *History of the Great Lakes.* Chicago: J. H. Beers & Co., 1899.

"Marine Notes," *Chicago Inter-Ocean*, November 4, 1900.

"Marine Notes," *Cleveland Plain Dealer*, May 27, 1896.

"Marine Notes," *Cleveland Plain Dealer*, May 28, 1896.

Project ShipShape. *Ship Information and Data Record: Choctaw.* Great Lakes Historical Collection, Wisconsin Marine Historical Society, Milwaukee, WI.

"Struck the Bridge," *Chicago Inter-Ocean*, October 31, 1900.

"Turned Up," *Cleveland Plain Dealer*, October 22, 1895.

Untitled, *Cleveland Plain Dealer*, April 21, 1893.

Untitled, *Cleveland Plain Dealer*, April 22, 1893.

Untitled, *Cleveland Plain Dealer*, June 1, 1896.

Untitled, *Cleveland Plain Dealer*, June 5, 1896.

Untitled, *The Marine Review*, February 1916, 60.

U.S. Department of Commerce, Bureau of Navigation. *Merchant Vessels of the United States for the Year Ended June 30, 1916.* Washington, DC: Government Printing Office, 1917.

"Wind and Snow," *Cleveland Plain Dealer*, October 20, 1895.

"With a Crash," *Cleveland Plain Dealer*, May 21, 1896.

Mr. Plimsoll Finally Leaves His Mark on the Great Lakes

An Act to Amend the Coastwise Load Line Act, H.R. 11915, 74th Cong. (1935).

An Act to Promote the Welfare of American Seaman in the Merchant Marine of the United States; to Abolish Imprisonment as a Penalty for Desertion; to Secure the Abrogation of Treaty Provisions Thereto; and to Promote Safety at Sea, Bill No. 302, 63rd Cong. (1915).

Editors of *Encyclopedia Britannica*. "Samuel Plimsoll," *Encyclopedia Britannica Online*, https://www.britannica.com/biography/Samuel-Plimsoll.

"The Load Line," *Detroit Free Press*, April 13, 1888.

"Load Line on Steamers Is Advocated," *Detroit Free Press*, December 2, 1902.

"Plimsoll Mark Put on Great Lakes Ships," *New York Times*, February 21, 1936.

Thelen, D. P., "Robert M. La Follette," *Encyclopedia Britannica Online*, https://www.britannica.com/biography/Robert-M-La-Follette.

Untitled, *Port Huron Daily Times*, February 27, 1902.

Untitled, *Port Huron Daily Times*, December 4, 1903.

Brotherhood of the Muskegon Breakwater

Andrie, Stan, Bultema Dock and Dredge, letter dated September 28, 1976.

Boyer, Dwight. *True Tales of the Great Lakes.* Thunder Bay, CA: Thunder Bay Press, 1976.

Bruce, Colin J., Imperial War Museum, London, England, letter dated January 10, 1992.

Dawson, William, letter dated January 24, 1977.

Goodman, Harry K. Erie Sand Steamship Company, letter dated July 26, 1976.

Horsley, Joan, National Maritime Museum, London, England, letter dated December 12, 1991.

"Marine Freak," *Port Huron Daily Times*, September 22, 1902.

"Marine News," *The Scanner* 16, Toronto Marine Historical Society (October 1983), https://tinyurl.com/y53a6pvo.

Sensibar, David, Construction Aggregates Company, letter dated July 29, 1976.

Untitled, *Cleveland Plain Dealer*, November 19, 1927.

Untitled, *Cleveland Plain Dealer*, November 21, 1927.

Untitled, *Muskegon Chronicle*, September 27, 1930.

Untitled, *Muskegon Chronicle*, September 29, 1930.

Untitled, *Muskegon Chronicle*, October 1, 1930.

Untitled, *Sandusky Register*, May 3, 1925.

Untitled, *Sandusky Register*, August 14, 1925.

Untitled, *Sandusky Star Journal*, May 2, 1925.

Untitled, *Sandusky Star Journal*, May 4, 1925.

Untitled, *Sandusky Star Journal*, May 5, 1925.

Untitled, *Sandusky Star Journal*, May 6, 1925.

Untitled, *Sandusky Star Journal*, May 7, 1925.

Untitled, *Sandusky Star Journal*, May 8, 1925.

Untitled, *Sandusky Star Journal*, May 9, 1925.

Untitled, *Sandusky Star Journal*, May 11, 1925.

Untitled, *Sandusky Star Journal*, May 14, 1925.
Untitled, *Sandusky Star Journal*, May 16, 1925.
Untitled, *Sandusky Star Journal*, May 18, 1925.
Untitled, *Sandusky Star Journal*, May 28, 1925.
Untitled, *Sandusky Star Journal*, May 29, 1925.
Untitled, *Sandusky Star Journal*, June 4, 1925.
Untitled, *Sandusky Star Journal*, June 11, 1925.
Untitled, *Sandusky Star Journal*, June 13, 1925.
Untitled, *Sandusky Star Journal*, June 18, 1925.
Wright, Richard J., Director, Northwest Ohio Great Lakes Research Center, letter dated September 2, 1976.

The Ghosts of Philo Parsons

Bowen, Dana T. *Memories of the Lakes*. Thunder Bay, CA: Thunder Bay Press, 1946.
Dunbar, Willis T. *Michigan: A History of the Wolverine State*. Grand Rapids: Wm. B. Eerdmans Publishing Co., 1995.
Obituary of Philo Parsons, *Detroit Tribune*, January 24, 1896.
"Tales from a Civil War Prison: Lieutenant Colonel John W. Inzer," *Archaeology Online*, last modified August 30, 1999, https://archive.archaeology.org/online/features/civil/words/inzer.html.
Untitled, *New York Times*, February 22, 1875.
Untitled, *Toledo Blade*, September 21, 1864.

The Blue Waters of the Juniata River

Bowen, Dana T. *Lore of the Lakes*. Thunder Bay, CA: Thunder Bay Press, 1940.
Brough, Lawrence A. *Autos on the Water—A History of the Great Lakes Automobile Carriers*. Columbus, OH: Chatham Communications, 1987.
George G. Sharp, Inc. "Marine Systems Analysis and Design," http://www.georgesharp.com (site discontinued).
Havighurst, Walter. *The Long Ships Passing—The Story of the Great Lakes*. New York: Macmillan, 1964.
"Juniata." *Historical Collection of the Great Lakes*. Bowling Green State University, https://greatlakes.bgsu.edu/item/436091.
"Juniata Is Satisfactory," *Detroit Free Press*, May 11, 1905.
"Laughlin Hits Juniata," *Detroit Free Press*, December 20, 1911.
Mansfield, J. B. *History of the Great Lakes*. Chicago: J. H. Beers & Co, 1899.

"Marine News," *Detroit Free Press*, May 16, 1912.

Project ShipShape. *Ship Information and Data Record: Juniata*. Great Lakes Historical Collection, Wisconsin Marine Historical Society, Milwaukee, WI.

"Tionesta's Sister Ship," *Detroit Free Press*, December 18, 1904.

"Twin Boats Side by Side," *Detroit Free Press*, May 15, 1905.

Untitled, *Port Huron Daily Times*, February 20, 1905.

Untitled, *Telescope* 20, no. 2, March/April 1971.

Index

N

O

Y